Becoming
SAVAGE

BETRAYAL RELEASED THE BEAST IN ME

NICHOLE ELLINGTON

BECOMING SAVAGE by Nichole Ellington

Published By: I Investments LLC, Chicago, IL 60643

www.nicholeellington.com

© I INVESTMENTS LLC

For Permissions: booking@nicholeellington.com

Book Design by HMDpublishing

ISBN: 978-0-578-83340-8

TABLE OF CONTENTS

PART THREE: BECOMING SAVAGE

INTRODUCTION

*Y*ou are about to read one of the hardest books that I have ever endeavored to write. It was hard because I had to remember things I was trying my hardest not to remember. But lesson number one is that avoidance doesn't bring about healing. I am so excited about releasing my story and sharing the lessons I was privileged to learn. People don't look at pain as a privilege, but really, pain is a blessing. Without the presence of pain, we would never know when something has gone haywire in our bodies or our spirits. Pain is not from the enemy. It is a gift from God. It is a part of His great design. Without pain, we would be destroyed and unaware it was happening. Since giving my life to God, I have told Him to let His will be done in me. Experiencing painful betrayals brought about God's will in my life. So, I am thankful.

While writing this book, I prayed and prayed that God would help me write it, and that He would heal many hearts, and change lives forever. This is not a "Tell All" book. It is, however, a "Tell Some to Empower ALL" book. My intention is not to hurt, harm, or disrespect anyone. If I ever felt like I was in my feelings (which happened), I stopped and prayed. When I got to the sensitive parts of my story that involved other people, I stopped and prayed. I only wrote what He allowed me to write. I've never written a book so carefully in my life. Why? Because I felt the gravity and weight of revelation and deliverance that can come to those who hear what God has to say through my story. So, know that what you will read changed my life forever, and it can do the same for you.

PART ONE

The Dimmer

CHAPTER ONE

Prologue: Thanksgiving Night

(The Blowup)

I stood there in the dining room looking into the living room. I was trying to stare subtly at my husband meshing and hanging out with my family. You see, sometimes it can be uncomfortable connecting and hanging out with your spouse's family. I understood this. They never did anything to make him feel uncomfortable; it is just hard to feel like you belong. However, this Thanksgiving he looked so natural with them. It is not easy trying to steal looks AND not look like a crazy person while doing it. Considering how terrible things had been for me, this was so good to see. I was just happy that something felt right for once.

Things had been tough for me. I was having way more bouts of anxiety than I had before. I had this weird sense that things were not right. It just wasn't well in my soul. And to top it all off, my health was failing me. I was chronically exhausted, having nausea, mental fatigue, and headaches all the time. I thought things were going to be looking up for us, because of our new jobs at the church. I felt like, maybe, now we could have some stability all round. I figured life would be less stressful without worrying so much about money. I felt content in thinking that that had to be the source of the issues.

It was getting late, and I was trying to do better at knowing when to leave, so I started to initiate the "it's time to go" sequence. "Go put on your shoes!" I told my son, so we could get this ball rolling. I already knew it was going to take a few reminders before we could actually get out the door. We rounded up our three-person family, and hugged and kissed all the people goodbye. I sat in the car pleased with how the night went. It was a successful Thanksgiving including some yummy to-go plates.

As I walked into the apartment, dropping my shoes off at the door, I began to contemplate how the food we brought back could fit into the fridge. Have you ever seen a fridge that looks average, but really has the least amount of space in it? That was our fridge. My thoughts wandered to my son. He needed to go straight to bed before he could get a chance to fully awaken past the sleepiness he got from the 15-minute car ride home. While I continued to try and figure out the configuration of the food in the fridge, my husband went into the bedroom. We then switched, and I went into the bedroom, and he headed to the kitchen. I started changing my clothes on my husband's side of the bed because it is closest to the closet and drawers, and out of the corner of my eye, I saw my husband's phone light up. It was noticeable because he never leaves it open/unlocked.

Before I could look away I saw the name of my friend and career partner. What is that? I suddenly got that feeling in the pit of my stomach. I've felt this feeling before. I picked up the phone and kept looking back at the door, listening to the floors intently to hear if he was walking back to the room. I saw the word baby, and I quickly grabbed my phone to take pictures of this (I had been here before, I knew the deal). I began to scroll up and saw a casual plan for both of them to get divorced, and who would go first. I read about them starting their business and stacking their money. Their plan was then sealed by confessions that they were both serious about each other. They ended their messages with "I love you", and "I love you too". I heard my husband coming back, so I put down the phone and passed him to leave the room.

I texted my sister about how I think my husband is cheating on me and that I needed to come over; I also sent her the pictures. Then I texted my mentor and campus pastor (who had walked this road with us before). I knew that in order for me to not backtrack after the lies start to roll in, and in order for him to get help, I had to let someone know so there wouldn't be a way of escape. I was calm. It was an eerie calm, but I was calm. I began to quietly pack my things right in front of him. Not angrily, just calmly. I would pass by him and say, "excuse me," politely.

After about 10 minutes, my husband asked what I was doing. I told him I was packing. I think his heart sank. I'm pretty sure he noticed his phone was open, plus what it was open to, and was hoping I hadn't seen it. But I had, and I couldn't un-see it. He began to beg me to just talk about it. I told him, I didn't have anything to say. I picked up my son, so we could leave, and he begged me to talk for just a few minutes. I still had a calmness inside of me, so I agreed to just listen. I sat on the couch across from him as he gave me an explanation that I didn't believe. Everything inside of me was craving to ask questions and to express my anger, but my resolve was to say nothing. I was fighting to handle this, not just differently, but to do it right. I think in some very tiny, small way, I was re-lieved. Why? Because for 12 years, I felt trapped in small doses of misery. A misery that was hidden well, "safely" in my head.

Well, I kept my end of the bargain. I sat and listened. Finally, he said he would leave, so that my son and I wouldn't have to. I agreed. I did not fall apart, I didn't even cry, initially. I just went straight to work. My first thoughts sounded like "What do I need to do?" ... "Where am I going?" ... "How much money do I need?" However, when he left, things got worse for me, because I became terrified. Fear began to grip me with all the possibilities you would see on an episode of a 20/20 special. I was not just scared; I was terrified of him coming back and doing who knows what. So, I got up and locked the bolt lock. It wasn't a fear that came from me thinking he was capa-ble or wanting to do something crazy, it came from not knowing what desperate people would do. It came from the insecurity you get when someone can comfortably live with you in a lie. You can laugh, eat meals together, go to work together, all the while carrying on a relationship with your partner's closest friend at the time. I was terrified. I wish I could say that that was the end of my night but it just kept getting worse and more traumatic for me.

I was determined to get out of there before he came back, so I began to pack everything I thought I needed. I packed toys, books, and clothes. Then, when I thought I was finished, I got a notepad, and I laid on the bed because I was going to come up with a survival plan. I am the type of person who loves writing things on paper, in tons of notebooks, and making lists. I'm a planner. I had it in my mind that tonight I was going to come up with a plan for how things were going to go from here. I like to know what the plan is at any given moment. I function better that way. I laid there with the notepad, and I couldn't think of what to do. I had nothing. That... is when I cried.

He texted and called. I listened more. One part of me was terrified, and the other part was concerned for my husband, hoping that his blood pressure did not increase like it did a couple weeks before. He told me that he was starting to have the symptoms of his blood pressure increasing to dangerous levels. I was panicking. I called the police and tried to get him help, but he was no longer where I thought he was. Then I tried to figure out where he was, and I called the police again, but he said he would take himself to the hospital nearby.

My goal was to leave by 6am to go to my sister's house. The process of running to get my car from the street and bring it to the back of my building was terrifying. I packed up the car and just waited for morning. I was literally watching the time as I waited. After all the crying, and that was mostly because of the amount of palatable fear that I was experiencing, there was no way I could sleep. I didn't dare sleep at all. He texted me, wanting to at least say goodbye to our son. I knew it was a bad idea, but I agreed. I wasn't trying to be cruel. I was trying to do the right thing for us...which was to leave.

He got into the back seat with my son, and began to cry, and kiss him. He was completely broken. It was terrible to see. I began to have tears stream down my face, but I kept staring forward and just wiped them away. This was too much!! This sitting, bubbling over hurt, begging and weeping went on for a long time until it was clear that there was going to be no change in my course of action. I pulled off, thinking about how my son would remember this morning in the car years from now. While everything was happening in the car, my son just looked like a mixture of confused, concerned, and oblivious to the gravity of what was happening at that moment. We got to my sister's house and my son and I laid on the couch, so we wouldn't wake anyone up. I was embarrassed, exhausted, and right back where I had just thought that things were looking up for our family.

My mother was in town for Thanksgiving this year. A few hours after we had been laying on the couches in my sister's living room, my mother opened the door to the guest room, walked out and noticed us. So, she came closer. I didn't want to tell her of the trauma I was experiencing. I didn't have words. I just needed to rest in a place of peace. She looked in my direction a little puzzled. Before she went back to her room, she told me that at about 3am she woke up with me and Brenden on her heart, so she stopped and prayed for us in her room. It's crazy how while I was going through one of the toughest nights of my life, God already had someone warring for me in prayer.

CHAPTER TWO

Oh Canada

(My Upbringing)

It was the end of the 80's and I was in a new country, an unfamiliar town, with people that somehow seemed so different from the people I knew. My family of five just moved to Jamestown, New York from Toronto Canada. The foundational part of my life was spent in a BIG multicultural city. I spent my first years primarily surrounded by a rich Caribbean culture. Everyone I knew personally was West Indian.

Now, I admit, I grew up as a picky eater (still am), however, I did enjoy the house filled with scents of the Caribbean food. I was surrounded by all the familiar accents from the different islanders. I loved it when our church had potlucks. I can almost smell it now. Curry chicken, patties, Roti, rice, and hard dough bread (my favorite). When we went to the grocery store, we bought our milk in a bag, and our frozen juice in a can. It always seemed like no matter whose house we were at, they had the same types of orange, green, or cream plastic jugs in the fridge, and the house décor was pretty much the same. You knew you were going to see beads hanging in the doorway frame of the kitchen, which created a pattern with rich brown wood and orange colors. You might go to the bookshelf or coffee table and find a bookend or some art carved out of wood. There wasn't a house I went into where they didn't immediately offer you some type of food. Hospitality was first and foremost.

Everyone I knew was from church, and they were all my "aunties" and "uncles". It was in one of those aunty or uncle's junior church classes, at the age of four or five, that I remember accepting Jesus as my Lord and Savior. I remember sitting close to the floor with the other kids in rows surrounding the teacher. They told us why Jesus came and died, and that we should accept His gift of salvation. That day, it made perfect sense to me. I loved my church! Every hymn we sang had a West Indian twist to it. This was all I ever knew. I was a little preacher's kid who lived in a big city engulfed in a rich culture.

Then we moved to a small town of around 35,000 people. To give some perspective, Toronto Canada, the city where I was born, had about 2.3 million people at that time. To say I had some culture shock, might be an understatement. It wasn't that the clothes or the language was different, but everything under the surface was different. How people acted was vastly different. What people would say and not say was too. These humans were different from the ones I knew where I was from. I used to be surrounded by a "hot culture," meaning a culture that was from a hot climate place, even though it was in Canada. Then there was a switch, not just in location but in culture. It was the real definition of culture shock.

In my eyes, I was an average kid who had a strict and loving upbringing. As a preacher's kid, I didn't feel any different from any other kid until we moved. Then all of a sudden, there was this distinction in my mind between me and the world.

Despite all the love in my house and my solid foundations, I was the little girl that would sit on the stairs on a Saturday by myself contemplating all of life itself. Weird. But it was normal for me. I had so much going on in my little head. I came from a place where, from my perspective, everything was perfect. It was not perfect, but I thought it was. My world got smaller and it made me much more aware of my surroundings. I was now living in a place where I could ride my bike out of the city limits with training wheels on. I was now living in a world where my best friend, from school, came to school with welts from being whipped. With a real horse whip!

I would go over to her house and her mom and brothers would be there. I loved visiting their house because often I would be offered an Éclair ice cream bar. You know, the kind on a stick which had chocolate at the center, it was covered in vanilla, then dipped in cookie crumble. They were just like the ones I got at school on special occasions. But after a while, her mom wasn't at home anymore. Her dad was already in jail when we met, but then her mom was gone as well. Her 14-year-old sister would come over to my home and learn how to cook mac and cheese, so she could take care of her sister and two brothers. These experiences and awareness made my world get a whole lot smaller. I would hear about all the cases of teenage pregnancy and drug use at the high school, and with each new bit of bad news, my world got a little bit smaller. I had a lot on my brain. My world had changed and quickly, my thought-life was full and never the same.

Four years later, we moved to Indianapolis, Indiana. I think I cried with tears of joy at the news of this change. I so wanted my world to get bigger again. I didn't know anything about Indianapolis. It could have been Timbuktu for all I cared. I just wanted a change. What I didn't know was that my analytical mind, my depressive and emotionally sensitive self, had nothing to do with where I was living. I didn't know it would pack its bags and move right along with us.

We moved to a place where there was more space. Eventually, I had access to more friends and more people. I wish I would have known that it only meant more people to please. You see, when you are as analytical as I was, more people meant more issues. My teenage hormones, on top of my overly analytical mind, created a two-scoop sundae that was already too much for me to handle. But when you add the bullying and constant messages from my peers that because I was "too dark skinned" I wasn't good enough, it was far too much. The message was loud and clear; I wasn't pretty enough and I wasn't going to be popular enough to be "chosen." I just wasn't enough for them. I soon adopted this doctrine like it was truth, and picked up some complexes that penetrated every area of my life. Now I had a three-layer sundae once you added the hopelessness. Oddly enough, in the midst of this time, I re-dedicated my life to Christ. I hadn't strayed from Him, but the level of hopelessness and weakness that I felt meant I needed more of God. This type of weakness and hopelessness had me hiding in bathroom stalls during lunch in middle school, and hiding in my father's office during church potlucks. Man, what a change! From the scents of West Indian food making me feel like I "belonged," to years later hiding in offices when it was time to come together to eat.

I graduated from high school and went to college, only to drop out three semesters later because I was so depressed. I found myself at a certain time of every month going from super excited to totally depressed. At times, I would literally close the blinds and huddle in my bed by myself. I was missing classes and assignments. It was either withdraw from all my classes or flunk out of college. So, I withdrew.

I thank God for mothers. They have such an intuitive nature about their children. For a while my mother had been marking in her calendar (where she put everything) all the times I was noticeably having issues. I finally went to the doctor and told her what I was experiencing. I was diagnosed with Premenstrual Dysphoric Disorder (PMDD).

Adding the sprinkles of my depression and so many more scoops and hidden layers made for a sundae that was way too much for me to handle. It was at this point that God met me at a women's retreat that my mother was hosting. He kick-started some healing in me that began with my self-esteem, and later expanded to my mind. I have been on a journey of healing, breaking habits, and acquiring tools to help me overcome the setup of my mind ever since.

One of my biggest struggles was my desire to please men. Because I accepted Jesus as my Savior at approximately age five, and rededicated my life to Him in middle school, my spirit had been battling my mind for years. To me, my mind was such a formidable opponent. My mind and the giant Goliath (from the Bible), had a few things in common. It was like an unstoppable force that seemed to have its own power. My mind's number one priority was to be accepted by people. Being accepted meant I had worth. My worth was wrapped up in what others thought of me. So, even though I really "loved" God, pleasing people was fighting for His throne in my life. I had such tremendous guilt and anguish within me, stemming from being super analytical. I knew what was wrong with me, and it tormented me that I was knowingly disappointing God. I wasn't bound by these issues, I just FELT bound by them. I didn't need to get saved again. When I got saved the first time...it took. The transaction went through. Lol. But my perspective and feelings had me blind to the truth that was so readily available to me.

CHAPTER THREE

The List

(How I Lost My Self-Esteem)

I moved from Canada (which to me meant my West Indian roots) to America. A lot of people move and migrate. This was normal. I think it is also normal for those who move to anywhere different from their place of origin, to experience a culture shock. I went from an environment of love, acceptance, and positivity from my community (based on my perspective) to rejection and negativity (based on my perspective) from my new community.

By the time I got to high school, I learned how to keep my head down and accept the rejection. My middle school experience was terrible, and I was made fun of at school and even by my friends at church. Everyone would talk about each other, and hone in on each other's insecurities. I made one solid friend in middle school who fully accepted me, and she was now my best friend in high school.

"The List"

One day, walking down the hallways of my high school during the passing period (which is in between classes) I was doing my best not to make it obvious I was looking for him. I already checked to make sure my makeup was right since I could only afford the cheap stuff that wore off after every class. I thought my outfit was cute, so I was set. I spotted him down the hallway. He was coming closer...I could feel the tension in the pit of my stomach, like the same feeling right before the big drop on a roller coaster. *Okay, I just need to look at him and smile. Don't look awkward before you look his way! Annnd look...I did it! Oh my gosh, he smiled back!!!!!!!* I could barely handle the tension in my stomach now because HE SMILED AT ME!

My best friend had a class with him, and she was going to try to get us together. She was a good friend.

Class was over, and I was rushing over to her class to catch a glimpse of him, but I missed him. It didn't matter anyway because I really just wanted to hear what my best friend had to say. I went into her class as she was packing her things up and she handed me a letter...a letter that he gave her in class. I was a little excited, but it was weird that she said she was "still" going to talk to him and try to get us together. I took the letter and walked to the front of the school and began to read that my butt and boobs are too big, I'm too this, and I'm too that. I was reading a list of everything my crush didn't like about me, and that he actually really liked my best friend.

I was reading this list of specific things, but just like Google translation, my heart read, "I'm not beautiful enough to be liked," it read "I don't have what it takes," "I can't get what I want if there is someone better around." Have you ever seen someone translate a short English sentence into another language and the translator goes on and on, and you think "why are they still going, it was a short sentence?" This is exactly what happened to me. It definitely was a list of everything my crush didn't like about me compared to my best friend (a terrible thing to do, and see), but my translation went above and beyond what I read.

After this incident, and many others, a shift happened in me...I became a quitter, a non-risk taker. A pattern of quitting before I could get rejected or further rejected arose. I had a "lay low" mentality so that I could never be embarrassed again. It took a lot to smile at him earlier that day. I was "putting myself out there," and I was horribly rejected.

I internalized that I was second best. I thought I didn't have what it takes to be "chosen and accepted." As a result, I would accept boys and men (and eventually married a man) simply because...they "chose" me. I accepted them even if they treated me as if I was second best. My subconscious mission was to prove that I was enough. I know I'm not the only one that has signed up, unknowingly, for this mission.

"The Beauty Breakthrough"

I mentioned before that I dropped out of college because I was depressed and had stopped engaging in school. Well here I was...back home...living with my parents again. Mommy invited me to go to a women's retreat she was hosting. I didn't want to go, but I went anyway, since my friend was going. It was time for service. I mustered up what I needed to go downstairs and sat down to hear the guest speaker, Minister Donna Hall. After she spoke, she began to minister to individual people. There was a line of people standing in front of her. I had seen things like this on tv, but I never experienced the gift of prophecy or Word of knowledge before. So out of wild curiosity, and a deep need for some help I got in line for her to speak what she felt God was saying to her about me. I normally would have been too embarrassed to stand in line. I would have been thinking waaay more about what others would think of me. Like, "do they see something is wrong?" or they'll think, "yea I know about them preacher's kids." But I was desperate and was too low to care that day. I stood there watching her as she spoke what she felt God was saying to her about different people to encourage them. I'm next. I stepped up and she paused. She didn't do this with all the other people. She just stood there, paused. I'm thinking "why isn't she saying anything". All of a sudden, she began to sing, "You are so beautiful to me, can't you see? You're everything I hoped for, you're everything I need, you are so beautiful to me." That was it. It was a wrap. God got me! I began to weep because God was expressing His acceptance of me. Only God knew that I didn't believe I was beautiful and couldn't even say those words out of my mouth. This was the hidden issue of my heart.

"The Philip Era"

Knowing that God had accepted me meant I could do anything, so instead of laying low, I began to step out some. Having the acceptance of God, radically changed my heart and my mind. I experienced a level of freedom from some of the chains that I allowed in my mind. I was freer to be me. This led to me moving to Chicago by myself where my sister lived and finding a group of people who accepted me for me. We did awesome things as a group. We produced a musical, recorded music and albums, created visions for future business plans...all as a group. I call this the "Philip Era." Philip was the musical genius that the group followed (so to speak). We didn't really follow him, but somehow it seemed like he was the epicenter of our creative world. We believed, like Captain Planet, that "with all powers combined" we could change the world with our music, ministries, and businesses. We found our purposes to be connected to his.

But then, one night after serving the youth and listening to him lead worship for the students, I headed home. It was a normal night. I got in my apartment and laid on the bed, ready to get on the phone and start talking about how the night went with the guy who became my future husband. I opened my phone to see message after message coming in. Phillip was hit by a drunk driver. He was on his way to have a date night with his new wife.

For about a month or so, we prayed and fasted for Phillip to be healed. We reached out to others to pray and had a special prayer service. Someone who was just about to work with Phil, in music, drove down from Canada to Chicago just to pray with us for one night. After we began to see glimmers of hope in his condition, he passed on. He died, and we were lost. Not just from grief, because yes that grief was thick and heavy, but also because, seemingly, our dreams died with him. When he was alive, I started things and I finished them. I was living life boldly. After that era had passed, I definitely started things. I continued with my cosmetology adventures, I did a little music, and I was a serial entrepreneur. I started a bunch of things, BUT I hardly finished anything.

These were two phases in my life that I thought brought the final healing in my mind that I desired, but they weren't. The Beauty Breakthrough and the Phillip Era were just part of the healing that I needed in my mind.

"My Breakthrough Completed"

One day I started writing. I began writing down everything that I felt God was saying. This was when Philip was still alive, because I would walk into Church and he would ask me how my writing was going. We were really seeking God so intensely, and individually. Several of us would be at church or somewhere by ourselves just to worship God alone and talk to Him in prayer. We would intercede for others in this private place. So, it was normal to run into him at the church during the week while he was either "maxing" on a ton of food (and a liter of orange pop just for himself) or catch him worshipping and even recording a few precious times with the Lord.

At the time, I was reading Psalms 139 and writing. I was reading the Bible scriptures I felt God lead me to, and writing the words that bubbled up in my spirit. It was so invigorating and exciting to feel the leading of the Holy Spirit as the words I wrote were blowing my mind with revelation like someone else wrote it. Suddenly, I had an "aha" moment. God called me out, through the Bible verses, telling me that how I felt about myself was THEE issue.

I had a breakthrough when God showed me that He accepted me. Check! I had a breakthrough when I was accepted by people for who I was, and discovered my gifts and mission in this world. Check! But the one box on this list that was not checked off was "me" validating "me." I didn't believe in myself. I didn't think I needed to. I didn't think that how I thought towards myself and the self-talk that I had going on in my head was sinning against God. God showed me how I had to renew my mind by changing my thinking.

My aha moment triggered me to not only become a "doer" but also a "finisher." God's validation was what I needed, but before then I didn't believe it for myself… about myself. I began to pursue my passions, not only with the confidence that God accepted me and that some people would accept me, but I accepted myself and believed in me. If there wasn't an opportunity or space for me in the culture, I believed I could create one. Period!

So, I kept writing. I published my first book. I became a worship director at two churches. I became a publisher's assistant, and quickly moved up to become the education director for this hybrid publishing company. Before I left the company, I was the Chief Operations Officer. I also started my brand and business to help overwhelmed and stressed out people overcome their mind and walk out the will of God for their lives. I became a finisher. This doesn't mean that everything I started needed to be what I do for the rest of my life, but I stepped up to do what needed to be done in each season. Now I help others to move from being "hindered" to being "doers," and others to move from being "starters only" to being "finishers."

But all this was not as straightforward as it sounds. This is not a Disney movie with an enemy that gets defeated, and then they live happily ever after. I came to realize that, just because you have been healed doesn't mean you don't have residue. What is residue? It is what is left behind. There are many people that have been cured from a disease but were then left with the damage that the disease left behind in its wake. Have you ever noticed in some alleys how there are grooves in the road from years and years of people driving in the same spot? Or after a snowfall, you see how there is a path created by the tires on the highway because everyone has driven along that same groove. And when you begin to drive, you feel safer or more comfortable driving in the same grooves. This is because if you drive outside of them, you might slip and slide—the car would not be steady, predictable and comfortable. This is really how life is. When we have lived a life one way, in our minds for years, we create a groove that is hard to get out of. You can be set free by the truth but choose to drive in the grooves because of the fear of the unknown...because of lack of trust.

Would you take a moment to really think about your residue with me? I had to ask myself "have I ignored the habits that were left behind from when I had low-self-esteem?" Have you ignored unresolved hurts that were left behind because of your upbringing? Or what about the ways of thinking about people, certain people groups, men, women or authority figures that don't line up with what God says about them? We can even create our own theology about certain things because of being hurt, that is not in agreement with the Word of God. All of that was me. I made some good and some bad decisions after my breakthroughs, and I knew the truth about undealt with residue. I thought because "I knew the truth," and "I knew what to and what not to do," that I should be good.

"Happily Ever After" didn't come because of what I understood. There is a level of knowing that is really just understanding. We do need to understand things, and the truth. But I found out that there is knowing (understanding), and there is KNOWING. This level of knowing doesn't just go up, but instead it goes down. It is a DEEP knowledge and understanding of truth that takes root in your life and bears lasting fruit. The Bible talks about it. James 1:21 talks about getting rid of moral filth and evil, which, in this case is your old way of thinking about yourself and others. Then it goes on to tell us to humbly accept the Word implanted in us because it will save our souls (which is our mind, our will, and our emotions). It does not say that if we just get an understanding of the Word that it will save our souls. It says that it is the Word "implanted" that will save our mind, will, and emotions.

This is huge! Why? Because you may have thought there was no hope. You may have thought that you were just stuck in a pattern that wasn't changing. You may have thought those things for the same reasons that I did. Like some of you, I prayed and cried. I fasted, prayed and cried, and then pressed repeat. I knew the truth, but still my thinking just didn't seem to change. I told myself I am not going up to that altar not one more time for the same thing, because nothing is changing. James 1:21 is the best news ever if you relate to these circumstances, because there is a solution beyond just understanding. There is more that you can do. You can go ahead and get rid of the condemnation and lies that the enemy has told you since you couldn't get it right. We have to go beyond hearing the Word and understanding the Word of Truth, to it getting deeply implanted in our lives, so much so that nothing can remove it.

Jesus gave us a great example of this when He shared with a crowd the parable, or story, of the seed and the sower. This is found in three of the Gospel accounts of Jesus. It is in Matthew 13:1-23, Mark 4:1-20, and Luke 8:4-15. Take a moment to read it and meditate on it for yourself. But what it revealed to me confirmed what God told me in James 1:21. He basically described to the crowd how a sower was sowing or planting seeds. He threw some of the seeds on a path (which got eaten by birds), some on a rocky place (which sprouted, but was too shallow and got scorched by the sun), some on a thorny place (it grew, but so did the thorns and it got choked out), and finally, some on good soil where it produced 30, 60, and 100 times what was planted. After he shared this picture story, his disciples definitely needed a better understanding and Jesus shared what he meant by this parable.

Jesus explained to his disciples that the seed is the Word of God or message about the Kingdom. When it is "planted" on bad ground it will be snatched away from your heart by the enemy, because you didn't understand it (understanding is important). When you plant it in your heart and get excited, but it is pretty surface level, life will happen. And **when** it does and any trouble or persecution comes, you're done with it all. The Word can be planted and then worry takes over, and/or we are consumed by chasing the lies of wealth. That "almighty" dollar. And really that is the lie; that money is almighty or all powerful. That it can solve your problems. Financial wealth is not what is standing between you and peace, or between you and joy. You can have peace and joy without having a dime. Why? Because if you truly have a relationship with the giver and not the gifts, you become satisfied and content. But I digress. The last soil describes the person that doesn't just hear the Word but understands it. Not just knowing it, but KNOWING it. Meaning, the Word that is implanted will save your souls. You will "bear fruit"!

We know we are not talking about a low level of just understanding, because the second, and third soil, Jesus described, mentioned that they received the Word and got a level of understanding, but it wasn't deep enough. Real roots run deep and wide. When I say wide, I am referring to every area of your life, and not just your self-esteem, or your church life, family life, or just your relationship life, but ALL of your life. Matthew 22:37 says to "love the Lord your God with all your heart, all your soul, and all your mind." This leaves no room for areas of life that the Word shouldn't be rooted in. Let me connect the dots. Jesus said, if you love me, you will obey me. He also said that He is the Word. So, if you love God, you obey His Word, which is obeying Him. We can't love God but ignore His Word in areas of your lives. This can seem daunting. I already know. But we don't do this on our own, or in our own strength. It is the Holy Spirit that teaches us and makes us fruitful. If we are intentional, He will make the roots of His Word run deep and wide, and you can't stop the fruit of the "spirit" from growing in you.

As I share more of my story, I receive hope knowing that even after making mistakes and dealing with my residue tripping me up, I am and will always have success in Jesus. The Holy Spirit gets me right when I start to drive according to the groove and habits that I created before I knew the truth. The implanted Word literally saves my soul!

PART TWO:

"I'm Not Crazy"

CHAPTER FOUR

Unbecoming Together

For years I had been asking for the same thing for my birthday. Two nights away in a hotel by myself (well my family or friends could join the second night...maybe). I just wanted to be comfortable, on a comfortable bed, and watch or binge watch whatever I wanted to. This all started many moons ago when I was single and just had had enough going on in my life. So, I just decided to drive out to Schaumberg, Illinois. I guess you can say it is a far suburb of Chicago. I got a hotel room and on the tv there just happened to be a marathon of NCIS. I went "ham" watching all the episodes back to back. IT WAS THE BEST! I really enjoyed myself. I was able to laugh as loud as I wanted, get up and dance how I wanted (with or without music). I could just be me without worrying if someone thought what I said or did was corny, cool, or not. Ever since then, that has been my desired "go to" for mental relaxation. But the way my life was setup, that couldn't happen like it did when I was single. The money was funny, and my time between family, working multiple jobs, and doing ministry was almost non-existent.

So, when my husband told me that he wanted to send me and my co-worker/friend away to a women's conference (which I heard was amazeballs) I was ecstatic. A get-a-way just for me never happened, but this was going to be great.

So, we went! I picked her up, we stopped for Starbucks, and then we hit the road. Road trips are a great way to learn more about people, because all you have is time to talk and enjoy music. And that was just what we did. We talked about pretty much everything, our past lives, husbands, and families. It was great conversation, and we got to know each other better.

We were an unlikely match because our personalities were different, but over the years, we both changed (as life does for everyone), and in this new season of life we meshed well. We didn't take much from each other, but we did add to each other's lives. It was a no drama friendship. That was my favorite part. There was no unhealthy demand or expectations from each other, which allowed for us to grow. And on this trip, we grew closer.

I had been praying for God to send me "my person." I even told my campus pastor about it and he was praying for me as well. I was looking for a friend that I could truly be one hundred with. I'm talking about the friend who is okay with "carefree hotel me". I used to have that, but my closest friend ended up back stabbing me. I lost that friend right before all the major milestones in my life (getting married and having a child).

I considered that maybe this might be that person, but there was some reservation there I couldn't figure out. When we got to the amazing hotel and chilled in the room, we talked more. And as I shared, I felt resistance in me to just say exactly the things in my heart. I would only allude to what had been going on over the years with me before and during my marriage. Part of the hesitation was embarrassment for the things I allowed and feeling like I would probably be judged.

At one point, I played this song that my husband had introduced me to called Hunger by David and Nicole Binion. The whole atmosphere in that hotel room shifted and the presence of the Lord was there. We could hardly say anything. Then when I opened my phone, it automatically started playing an Instagram story from the founder of the conference and it was her daughter singing the same exact song. It was so unreal. I knew then for sure that this conference was going to be life changing.

Throughout the conference, God was just encouraging me, and I was being changed. He was preparing me for the future, without me even knowing it. I began to let my guard down with this friend and co-worker. This time that we spent together brought us much closer than we had been. Much closer than boss and employee.

Our business dealings together started off with her frequently mentioning how she was praying for someone to come and help her with her business. After I spent time praying about it, I offered my help. It turned into building together and getting the company on the right track and prepared for greatness. There was only a bright and successful future ahead.

In the course of our time working together, we had two prophecies given to us. One was at a ministry event about prayer, and the second was at our biggest event together by the keynote speaker. I couldn't have imagined that the same day that we received the last prophecy was the same day (I was told) that sparked the wrong turn in the conversations between her and my husband.

CHAPTER FIVE

Manipulation Fest

The first time I went back home to the apartment, I didn't know what I was going to say if my husband was home. I needed to pick up a few things, and I had in mind to take a shower while I was there. Before I could even get into the apartment my heart was beating fast. But I was steadfast and stronger, as well as clearer than I had ever been before. My husband was there in bed, and we had a conversation. It was a calm one. His appearance was one of someone who hadn't slept for days. One that was hiding out from everyone that might now hate him or protecting himself from anyone that might have been threatening him.

We talked. This time, I shared where I was at and what I would and wouldn't do. I told him that I wasn't going to divorce him, but that we were absolutely separated. I told him how I didn't want to work on the marriage at this time, and that our marriage had blown up—it needed to be. It needed to be because Thanksgiving wasn't an event. It wasn't a one-time unfortunate thing that happened. It was game seven of our finals. It was a bomb that finally went off, and that was a good thing. I had no intentions of rebuilding or seeking restoration. The whole foundation of our marriage was based on brokenness, insecurity, low self-esteem, and a LOT of manipulation. I didn't want to restore that! We needed what we never had. Plus, it was necessary for us to become healthy enough to handle each other in marriage. We were not ready for that.

"This Is Us"

Our marriage was trash from the beginning. Wow, that was intense! Let me make sure I'm clear. The people in our marriage were not trash, but the marriage was. My relationship with my husband included laughter and watching movies and tv together. We have had great deep conversations. We have supported each other in different ways over the years. But this is not enough for a marriage without other key elements and a solid foundation. Also, even though these good things were in our marriage, the bad things that were mixed in made the marriage toxic. Keep in mind, you can dress trash up, you can cover trash, and even get used to the smell after a while, but that doesn't redefine it. It was still trash. It was an amalgamation of mixed up thinking, hurtful decisions, checking out emotionally, rejections, lies, numbness, indifference, giving up hope, and more trash. It was all of these things ultimately because I allowed myself to continue on in a relationship with someone who "kind of" liked me and didn't really want "me for me." The real me.

I wasn't enough. All these years, before we even got married, I knew better. I knew this truth. I would bring it up, how I wasn't going to be second to anyone, and not on anyone's list. But the truth is, I allowed myself to be on the list, because the Word wasn't deeply rooted. Some of my trials looked like feelings that I wouldn't find someone else to love me, or feeling like I would be stepping out of the will of God to leave. These trials plucked up some of the seeds of truth in me, and scorched others. I had residue that I never dealt with from going all the way back to the list. I had created a groove of coming back, no matter how I was treated, honestly—because I had put so much into this relationship (or really, put up with so much). It was uncomfortable to drive outside of the groove.

When you ignore the truth and keep going, you end up being responsible for staying in the position to get hurt. This in no way excuses the actions of anyone else, but if I was walking in who God fully created me to be, a woman of virtue with standards, I wouldn't have been around to get the "punch in the gut". I wouldn't have been around for the bomb.

The day we got married, everything changed. We were now one. No turning back. I was excited, but I also suffered from the "he will change once we are married" syndrome. On our honeymoon, there was an incidence where I was rejected, and that was a blow for my motivation to be an amazing wife. The rest of the honeymoon sucked, terribly. Mainly because there was so much disappointment already for what I thought marriage would be for us. I thought that if I was the adventurous sexy wife, who offered my husband to be first in everything, that all would have been well. I was the one who would sign cards making sure I put his name first. I gave him first pick on which side of bed to sleep on, and always let him dictate what we watched on tv. When we first got married, I almost ruined my feet walking to the grocery store, because I was determined to get that meal cooked for my husband. Only problem was, I didn't have on the proper shoes for that type of walking and messed my feet up for a month!

If you look at the wife I became after a little while, you would never think that that was how I started off. Most of those things I kept up, but after I experienced a couple of really bad situations within my marriage, all related to how I wasn't enough, I shut down to power saving mode like on my phone. When you turn on this mode on your phone, you can only use it to do the essentials in the most basic ways. That was me. I barely cooked anything (which was never a good thing for me), barely kept up our apartment. I was down to the essentials. I wouldn't deny my husband, and I tried to be the best mother to our son. If anything was wrong, I was there. With the little heartbeat that I had, I still mustered up strength to try to "fix things." Journals, challenges, I even tried to get us to pray daily together several times. Everything you would hear in a marriage group, session, or video, I would try to implement. Even if it was secretly. Some things we tried, and some things were met with repeated rejection or put in the holding pattern of "I'll think about it" or I'll let you know". I think I hated the holding pattern the most.

Why was I rejected? Why was I not enough? Well guys, most of you have heard the saying, and probably don't want to hear it, but it is true. "Hurt people, hurt people." Saying that and knowing that doesn't make any of the hurt less painful, and it doesn't magically erase traumas, but it does cause you to realize that where there is a cause there is hope. If there is a cause, it can be discovered and healed, but it is a choice that individuals have to make.

My husband wasn't a monster. My eyes were always opened to the greatness within him. He handled us getting pregnant within a month of marriage very well. He actually excelled. He cooked and cleaned and got groceries. He has always been a hard worker. He stayed working and would go to work early to chat with his co-workers about God. He was and is a man of vision and GREAT calling. He is a watchman. He foresees things to come before anyone else could even imagine it. He is a great father. He is faithful to our son, and we both continue to grow as parents. In our marriage, he would do things like bring home a candy bar or chips that I like or come home and tell me to get dressed because we were going out to the movies. Of course, these made it to social media because I wanted to affirm his greatness. Even good people are not totally one thing or another. We are not perfect people. But unresolved hurts, childhood and past traumas, curses spoken by others and by oneself will cause one to drive in the groove. When the truth is not rooted deep and wide of who you are in Christ, it doesn't matter what she or he said, and regardless of what they did, you drive in the groove. You end up going back to old habits. It is safe there. There is a weird sense of validation there.

Our marriage had to blow up to make room for healing. If our funk didn't hit the fan, I probably would have never gotten free of my chains. We needed C4 explosives to tear up what we built on sinking sand. We were so deep in our grooves that we couldn't get out until the bomb went off. But with the bomb comes the reaching, grasping, and desperation, which brought about a "manipulation fest" (as my husband called it).

"Trauma AGAIN"

It was Sunday morning and I was dreading going to church or doing anything. Although church had always been a place of refuge for me, at that time it was also the place where all three of us worked together. I was still in somewhat of a shock from what had happened just days before on Thanksgiving. I was laying on my sister's air mattress next to my mother's bed which held my mom and my son, because he wanted to sleep on the big bed with Grandma. I started receiving text messages from my mother-in-law about my husband regarding her concern for his emotional state. She was going to go and check on him. I had to fight my first thoughts, cast them down and I just prayed and gave it to God. I had to stay out of my feelings, because I will always answer to God for my actions. Even though people would have thought it to be okay to have an attitude, a few choice words and so much more when it came to this whole situation, I refused to become something I am not because of other people's choices. And God's grace IS still sufficient if we receive it. Sometimes we don't want God's grace because we WANT to allow our flesh to have a moment. If there was ever a time I might have wanted to act out in my flesh, and the world would have been okay with it, that was the time. But when the Word is deep and wide, you produce good fruit instead.

After a while, I received another text that my mother-in-law couldn't get into the apartment with her key. He had locked the second lock. I had to throw some pants on and drive over to our apartment. I had to move quickly because she told me that he had sent her texts that had suicidal language. As I drove to our apartment, I prayed and cried the whole time. Walking up to our outside front door, I prayed and braced myself because I didn't know what I was going to see. My heart was literally beating fast as I unlocked the door and took each step into the apartment.

I entered our bedroom only to find my husband half under the bed, crying and saying how sorry he was. He looked as though he was experiencing complications with his blood pressure. I asked him what symptoms he was having, and it lined up with a hypertension attack, so I decided to call 911. The fire department came fairly quickly, but my husband refused to go with them. They asked us to leave the room. I stepped into the space in front of the bathroom and that's when I noticed a T-shirt tied into a noose wedged into the door way of the bathroom. I immediately started crying again. I kept thinking, *"Are you serious!?! Is this really happening?!"*

When one of the firemen came to tell us that he was refusing to go, I showed him the noose and told him about the text messages. They then informed him that since he had sent those texts, he didn't have a choice. He got dressed and we left to walk to the ambulance. My husband was visibly upset but not from the hurt or his heart racing. My first thought was to get in my car and meet them at the hospital, but I jumped in the car with my mother-in-law. I know this must have been hard for her to see and experience, to get those messages, and to see her son like that on the floor. But she was strong, and we kept it moving. We arrived at the hospital slightly before the ambulance—as we stood at the door the ambulance was parking. They put him in a wheelchair which is standard and according to the rules. But I was confused because as he got closer and closer, I noticed that he and the paramedic were laughing together, like they had been having a ole good time. We headed in and they took him to a triage area. They hooked him up to check his vitals, and of course, his blood pressure was through the roof.

This whole time at the hospital was such a roller coaster of emotions. I was sitting there listening to all the jokes with the nurses and the laughter between them, and I was the one questioned as to why I did this, and who I told. I was made to feel like this was all my fault. It was like I was in la-la land. Was I really being presented as the one who was going to make him lose his job? Apparently I was at fault for asking for prayer and keeping my campus pastor/mentor (and supporter of our marriage through the years) updated on when I found my husband under the bed, and the suicidal messages. I was traumatized, but somehow, I was being portrayed as the one "at fault." At one point my knee was just shaking. I was in disbelief of what world I was sitting in, in my head. I almost got sucked into this alternate universe and laughed at a couple jokes. I listened as my husband explained that all of this was to get me and my son back home. He told the nurse that he knew that if he sent the texts to his mom, then turned off his phone that she would call me, and we would come. The noose was a part of the plan as well. I sat through the explanation, and the jokes, and then it hit me...What in the world is going on here?!?! I couldn't leave because I left my car, and I couldn't get reception on my phone to call someone to come get me. I had to remind myself over and over, "I'm not crazy!"

"I'm Not Crazy"

I made it through Thanksgiving night, and here I was laying on the couch, waiting for a decent hour, to get up and move about. When I found the messages during the night, I immediately sent a message to my sister, and to my campus pastor. I knew that if I didn't send it to him, I would find a way to eventually get back in the groove and cover up everything so we could get back to "normal."

Not this time. I had been there before. This was the final straw that was going to break this camel's back.

When my mother was done with her morning devotions, I asked if she could watch Brenden while I went out for a while. I had not told my mom what had happened, but she knew it was serious and that I was broken. As I got into the car, I received a text from "her". I could tell by the text that she wasn't sure how much I had seen in the messages between her and my husband. I didn't have anything in me to deal with that in a holy and righteous way. I had to go sit with my campus pastor and his wife. As I walked through their door, I was shaking my head, but when I sat down, I couldn't keep the tears from flowing, even though I was trying. I didn't want to be hurt by this. I wanted to be strong. I went through my night and shared what had happened, and as I talked, it was like God was speaking through me. I would share feelings, but then truth would come out of my mouth. Clarity would come out of my mouth. As I talked, I asked out loud what could be done for me to trust again, that we haven't already done. Then the answer followed and I said "time and counseling". These were the two things that would be different than any other time when we walked this same road.

As I spoke and dumped out all the feelings and truth, something important stumbled out of my mouth. It started off as a statement, but then it turned into something from God, something I had to hide in my heart so I wouldn't go back to driving in the groove. I said, "I'm not crazy." It was like those words were highlighted and underlined in my spirit. I had to repeat it. I felt the Holy Spirit when I said those words. Even in that moment, I thought to myself, *I am going to have to write a book called "I'm Not Crazy".* It ended up being a section instead of a book because it is not the whole story.

   When I coach clients, I talk about self-talk and how when we rehash and repeat the 10% of our lives that is bad, it ends up painting the whole 100%. So even though you possess 90% of blessings and good things, the 10% is all we see. Well, this is not that. "I'm not crazy" was incredibly powerful, and is still empowering me to this day, BUT this portion of survival, the trauma, plus what I have to do to heal and move from this kind of blow is not the whole 100%. The whole 100% is how I'm becoming savage. "I'm not crazy" is the reminder. Becoming savage is the victory. It is my redemption story, and it can be yours too.

CHAPTER SIX

How Did We Get Here?

Where is here? Well, for 12 years of my life I allowed myself to be talked into doing things I didn't want to do. I allowed myself to be ignored. Knowing that I was enough, I allowed myself to be treated otherwise. I use the term "allowed" because there was no gun held to my head. I wasn't physically trapped in bondage. But I was emotionally trapped in bondage. Because of fear, I stayed in unhealthiness. This seems like it is something that only happens to people who don't know who they are. But I knew. I allowed the behavior by simply staying, when I should have been leaving (before we got married). My relationship brought out the compromising side of me. Sometimes we think that since there are good times and laughs, and late-night conversations about the future, that everything will be fine regardless of the red flags.

I was the one who spoke up when I felt that things were not right or that I wasn't being treated right. We talked about everything. But when you want someone to stay, you'll agree to change. I was the one who didn't run away when I saw the ugly, and I thought that was my badge of honor. I thought it was my superpower. I was the ride or die. I didn't realize that that was a true statement, but it was more like ride and die.

What was my death? There was a death to my morals and commitments to God. I compromised so much. I did things I said I would never do. I wanted to do things I previously never desired because I allowed myself to be in atmospheres where desires like that grow. Also, when you spend so many years speaking up, but not taking any action, eventually you stop speaking because you know you're not going to do anything about it. I was in my right mind. I counted the right cost and decided to "live with it if it never changes." I literally talked to God about wanting change, but if it didn't change, I would just live with it. Do you understand how low your self-esteem has to be, to decide—before marriage—that you're going to "live with it?" I obviously didn't think that I deserved better. I didn't think that being lonely was better than being with someone I was living in pain with.

"Pathology of Betrayal"

Almost every year, towards the beginning of the year, at church we would have an event called the First Love Conference. It is a conference based on God being our first love. It had been about a month and a half since "Thanksgiving" (sidebar: I am redefining this holiday from pain to real thanksgiving). I was standing in the choir and we were singing the song "So Will I." This song just about wrecks me every time. And every time it seems that God just highlights a different line from the song to reveal His love for me. One of the first lines that got me was, "on a hill You created." It blows my mind that God created the Hill that His son was going to be later hung on. That is intentional, powerful love!! He saw His redemption plan through, just for us! However, this time it was a different line that got me. It was the last line that says, "you're the one, that never leaves the one behind." In that moment, it hit me. I was the one that was never left behind. As much as I don't like drama, or pain...and as much as God doesn't like it either, it seems like He knows just what we need to experience for us to truly know His love. That we can know it as much as humanly possible. I wept. I walked off stage and I couldn't stop weeping and weeping because I was the one. I was the one that God always stayed with. People have betrayed me over and over. People failed me over and over, but God...He never did. There was no pit of depression that God didn't get in with me. He never stopped talking to me and reminding me of His love. When I was betraying Him over and over, He never stopped loving me. This is why my worship is so fierce. It is because I've experienced a love that was so fierce, that I never experienced from any human EVER.

After I took my seat next to my husband, we listened to a word that was like God took a seat in front of me and had a one-on-one conversation with me, while "some man" was talking in the background. This preacher was a vessel, but it was God speaking to me. Only He knew my inner workings and thoughts. It was so powerful and needed, but what really took the cake was near the end. The preacher asked us to think about the past trauma and patterns that needed to be given to God. So, I did. I thought back and God revealed to me, in that moment, scenario after scenario going back to my childhood where I was betrayed or backstabbed by the ones closest to me. I couldn't believe it! I never saw this before. It was childhood friends, church friends, in middle school, high school, college, and repeatedly in my adulthood. Names were just coming to me. I didn't see this before and I just began to cry...again. But I wasn't crying because I had been hurt repeatedly. I was in AWE of God, how He could heal my heart so many times because I chose to forgive. I forgot all these times that I was hurt because I forgave them. Right now, I have friends who in the past committed horrible acts against me. I forgave them. I let them repent and grow, and if God wanted them back in my life, I let them. Of course, this is not the case for everyone, because everyone doesn't make those same choices to repent and grow. Not everyone should continue to be in my life either. But I allowed God to dictate that for me and not me for Him. It wasn't even intentional. I continued to be me because I was healed.

"How Did I Get Here?"

Through counseling and self-reflection, one can begin to see the left turns they brought on by ignorance, redefining experiences, and misguided thought processes. There are several mistakes or decisions that I made that got me to this place after 12 years. One being that I operated in two realms of either accepting disrespect or overlooking it. Some of that came from redefining the disrespect that I received. This is why I had to take pictures of the messages, and why I had to send them to the ones I trusted. I didn't want to give myself a chance to redefine the disrespect or redefine the situation to make it tolerable or livable.

Before we got married, I allowed myself to be used because I didn't have faith that there was better out there for me. My words at the time might have been, "God will take care of me, and I don't have to take this." But my actions exposed my real heart which said, "If I let him go, I might not get him back or find someone else."

How did I get here? I truly believed that God ordained us to be together. And I still believe that. I believe that it was the will of God for us to be husband and wife. But I realized that there was something I didn't think about. I didn't think about free will. Even though God has a will, and He delights in us seeking His will to perform it, He also gives us free will to make decisions for Him or against Him (or against His will). We can admire God but not want His will for our lives. I believed and I endured; these are good things, except when you find yourself sinning or ignoring the other things God is saying. Yes, His will was for him to be my husband, but it was not His will for me to compromise who I am in Christ or compromise my purity because He is supposed to be my husband. God doesn't just have a will for the future, but also for today. Here. Now.

Have you ever stopped to think about the pathology behind the things that you do? Have you discovered any patterns or even excuses that have led you to where you are now? Whether you're hurt or whole, as humans we have to take inventory so that we can discover what God is revealing to us in every season. One of my favorite scriptures is Psalms 139:23-24 which reads, *"Search me oh God and know my heart; test me and know my anxious thoughts. See if there is any offensive way in me and lead me in your way everlasting" (NIV).* Humbling yourself to pray this prayer will keep you at the feet of Jesus. It keeps the lines of communication open when it comes to our part. God shows us...US!

"Cracker Barrel"

I knew that Cracker Barrel was one of my favorite places to eat, but I never knew I would find some healing there. It had been weeks since everything went down, and we were on speaking terms because we have a son to take care of. One Sunday, I got a text from my husband asking if I wanted to go to Cracker Barrel to eat. It was weird because I believed that I was already planning on going there by myself. I agreed cautiously. You see, I had my mind made up about what I was and wasn't going to do, and my mouth was no longer shut, so I felt I could handle lunch as a family. Especially, since my son was a part of this experience.

I always order the same thing when I go to Cracker Barrel. I get the chicken and dumplings, two or three sides, and if I can afford it, two pancakes. And of course, I get the biscuits! However, this time, the conversation was not like the conversations that we usually had. We ate and sat in the Cracker Barrel for hours as my husband confessed to me all the wrong he had done to me. "See, I'm NOT crazy!" We then went into the car since we had already taken up a table for hours and spent another several hours in the car outside the Cracker Barrel in the parking lot.

The great thing about "funk" hitting the fan is that you are free to be yourself. Exposure seems like the worst thing in the world but one thing my husband said was that it brought freedom. He didn't have to uphold any personas, and he could just be real. One amazing gift that my husband got from this experience was love. In the worst possible experience, he found out what it is like for men to surround you and keep you held up at your lowest. These men were young and old, and committed to walking this out with him. During this season, he literally had a different man for each day checking in, having conversations, and going out for breakfast or lunch. He had to have the real and tough conversations that brought him to his "Search me oh God" moment.

As we sat in the restaurant and in the car, this man confessed everything to me. I am not talking about the most recent incident at the time, I'm talking about from the moment we met. He confessed how he did use me, and just kept me around until he wanted me again. He confessed about the emotional abuse throughout the years, the rejection, the abuse of silence and gas lighting, the unwillingness. He confessed how he took me for granted and what I brought to him before we were even married. Ya'll, HE CONFESSED! We were at Cracker Barrel from a little after 12 noon, until about 8pm at night. It was dark outside.

We talked some about what we wanted in a new relationship, because I wasn't playing about trashing the old one. It was like we were getting to know each other again. It was nice to talk about and dream about, but the real experience was the healing that came from those hours of confession. It was like all those years that I was made to believe that I was crazy was being washed away. The bondage of feeling like I was walking on eggshells in my own home and feeling like I couldn't say or do what I wanted or felt that I should do, was being washed away. I wasn't crazy. I didn't have to tell him what he did. He knew, and he confessed. He went all the way back to 2005 and it was now 2018. It really takes a man to admit his wrongs...for hours!

That night hope was born again. There was a glimmer of "this might be possible." That night I began to see how that one betrayal was beginning to be one of the best things that had happened to me.

CHAPTER SEVEN

How Could I For̲give... Again?

I can almost comfortably say that I'm a forgiveness "expert". That is funny to say, but when you have been given opportunity after opportunity to forgive, and you take it, you learn a few things. This question of how I could forgive, and more importantly forgive "again," is a common one. I can hear some of you now saying, "I might be able to forgive once, but not again...and again." I honestly can say I get it. These are valid feelings. If they weren't valid, then people in the Bible wouldn't have felt the same way. But they did. Peter felt like you and I feel. Peter straight up asked God how many times should we forgive and He gave a number I'm sure sounded pretty big. Jesus' response to him was to forgive 70 times seven, signifying as many times as needed.

I believe we struggle with the 70 times seven concept, because we have a skewed view of forgiveness. When you look up the definition of forgiveness, you get two definitions. The first one is what most of us think is expected of us and seems virtually impossible. The first definition describes not being angry anymore or not being upset at someone for what they did to you. This is not the forgiveness that Jesus was talking about. He wasn't talking about emotions. Emotions come and go based on what happens to us. Emotions are reactive. Forgiveness is not based on what emotions we feel.

The second definition says to cancel a debt. This is the type of forgiveness that we are supposed to follow. Jesus talks about it when he was teaching us how to pray in Matthew 6:12 which reads, "and forgive us our debts, as we also have forgiven our debtors" (NIV). We live in a restitution society. We live in the "I've been working for you for years and you do me dirty...YOU OWE ME!" type of society. We believe in an eye for and eye. In other words, when you take from me, you owe me. If you hurt me, you owe me. This is Biblical, but that eye for an eye was from before Jesus came and changed the game for us. It was before Jesus ushered in grace into our lives by paying the price for our sin/debt ONCE and for ALL. The type of forgiveness that Jesus requires of us now is releasing debt. It is acknowledging a debt and then canceling it. It is not redefining the debt. It is not acting like the debt never happened. You cannot cancel a debt that never existed. It IS relinquishing a debt officially and not making one pay that debt anymore. It is not based on whether they deserve their debt to be released or have stopped racking up debt.

This is so important for two reasons. One being, why would you want to be a hypocrite? If you have accepted

Jesus the Christ as your Lord and Savior, your debt has been canceled once and for all......ON CREDIT! Meaning, the mistakes you make now have already been paid for. But we still feel like another person's debt is worse than ours. "We are the exception to the rule, and our debt is not as bad as others." God didn't put a cap on how much sin He would forgive of ours, and we should not accept such amazing forgiveness if we are not going to give it amazingly.

The second reason for forgiving the debts people owe you, is because you can't be forgiven if you are not forgiving. This is not something to mess with. Do you really want someone else who has done awful acts against you, to stop you from being forgiven? That debt is not worth it. Don't go to jail because someone won't pay you back what they owe you. And that is another consequence of unforgiveness. You are the one paying the penalties when you don't release others from the debts they owe you. You become the one in chains emotionally. You can't go certain places, hear certain songs or be around certain people, because you won't release and cancel the debt. I mentioned earlier that I am redefining the holiday "Thanksgiving." I'm doing so because I have released the debts that were owed to me and I will NOT live in bondage and sadness every year because of what happened that night and in that season.

I'm not going to lie. Leading up to that next November... I felt it coming. I felt the dread rising up in me. I began to get a tiny amount of anxiety when I would even see the word November. But then I had to get a little "gangsta" in my spirit and rise up instead of sitting down and taking this. I will not allow my emotions to dictate to me how my holidays are going to be. This will not be my life. I see people surrendering all the time to their feelings. I don't have time for that. There are people who need to be free, who are waiting on my freedom. And I tell you the same thing. There are people who are waiting on you to become savage and rise up from your ashes and walk confidently in your authority. To walk out the ministry God has for you. You don't have time for this! Don't let unforgiveness be the reason someone who needs your gifts has to do without. They are waiting on you to be free. CANCEL THE DEBTS!!

When I forgive, I have the understanding that I may have to cancel several debts over and over. As you walk through tough experiences, you begin to discover new things that you need to forgive. And when you discover those things, you cancel those debts too. You may have noticed that I haven't talked too much about the feelings. Feelings are valid, and they are a gift from God. They can fuel you to step up and step out. They can make love so much richer. Feelings are great! They are also like nerve endings indicating to you when something is wrong and/or if you are in pain. It is because feelings are reactive. When someone steps on your foot, it is okay to say ouch. Why? Because it hurts. Forgiveness doesn't take from you the right to say ouch. And if someone goes as far as to shoot you and the bullets shatter some things, or does some damage in you; forgiveness doesn't take away your right to heal.

We often expect our debtors to fix us. But not everyone who shoots you is also a licensed doctor or surgeon. Not everyone has the capabilities to heal what they have broken. And we should not have those expectations of those who wound us. Many hurt people hurt people without degrees in psychology to fix it. If you have had this expectation from the ones who have hurt you, you should cancel that debt now as well.

Healing is important, so take yourself to the hospital. When you need healing, take yourself to an expert in the healing that you need. It is okay to say that you are not okay after someone metaphorically shoots you. Don't bleed out trying to be strong. Take the time to be healed. Don't move on without healing! Talk to your pastor or spiritual leader if they give sound Biblical advice and are good listeners. Go to a Christian licensed therapist. They can help you deal with the science of how our emotions work and get to the root of how you made your "grooves."

My process is this...I forgive immediately (I release the debt), then I go elsewhere for healing. These are two separate things. Forgiving, and healing are separate. Don't wait until you are healed to then forgive. Forgive, then go get your healing. Don't hold back YOUR forgiveness because you haven't forgiven someone else. And don't let the enemy lie to you to make you believe that you're not forgiving because you still feel hurt. I immediately forgave her, and him, and eventually them (we'll talk about who "them" are later). Then I went to seek healing. When you are healed, and as you are getting healed, you can better determine your next course of action with more clarity. Forgiving someone doesn't mean you have to stick around for them so that they can rack up more debts with you. That is not wisdom. And if someone is "sick" emotionally or spiritually, they may need to be in ICU or in isolation from you so that you don't contract what they have (or a mutated version of what they have, like bitterness). If you have been abused, you should forgive the debt, seek healing, and operate in wisdom and safety. You don't have to stick around for more abuse. It doesn't matter the type of abuse. This is not a requirement of forgiveness. Just release and cancel the debt. Everything else are separate issues that need to be addressed separately.

"Forgive Again, and Again"

Was it easy for me to forgive just because I had this knowledge? No! But it was doable. My mentor taught me that I can do hard things. And I would add that I can do hard things again and again, if they are necessary things. My life blew up. I mean, things were bad. Just because I forgave didn't mean everything was looking up afterwards.

So many things were stripped away from me. My marriage was stripped. My friendship was stripped. My career that I was building with "her" was now gone. My "pay the bills" job was also gone (then I got a portion of it back). The ministry that we were serving in was taken and a lot of the friendships were now changed or ended. My health was not good, and the stress was taking my hair out. I had to walk through the consequences of those actions.

After my husband was released from the hospital and after "manipulation fest", we were both called into a meeting. In this meeting were leaders and pastors, along with my four-year-old son. I listened as we both lost our jobs, and as my husband apologized and with tears repented. I was thoroughly bothered by the fact that this was happening in front of my son, and that it had more to do with my husband than anything to do with me. I had a lot of questions about what was happening that just irritated me.This brought about an offense in my heart for "them." Now I had to forgive again. These leaders meant no harm and was doing the best that they knew how to handle this situation, but their actions or inaction still brought about hurt. I was in for a journey of walking through the hallways at work, looking into the eyes of "them" and feeling some kind of way. But I was determined to fight to release their debt.

Yes, I experienced drama, frustrations, anger, wanting revenge, deep pain as a woman and mother, loneliness and hurt. But I also got to experience the blessings of it all. Without these aspects of my life being blown up like a bomb, I would have still been in bondage. I would not have sought after my healing and experienced the "come up" that God gave me.

When you forgive, then heal, you can learn to live with boundaries and faith. They CAN co-exist. This new relationship that I have with humanity is one of boundaries and faith. I am not jaded because I sought healing and grace. Now I can enter into relationships believing the best, while establishing boundaries at the same time. When the boundaries are not respected, I can healthily move right along. I can do this confidently without some attitude of bitterness or a chip on my shoulder from past experiences. I need grace, so I must extend grace. Grace can shift our perspective to see people properly. I don't need to hate you or continually be angry with you just because I have to set boundaries with you. It is me wanting the best for their healing, and for mine. It is seeking peace. This forgiveness might be new to you. You may have never realized that this is the forgiveness that is 70 times seven. This is the forgiveness that our "Good, Good Father" has prescribed for us. When we forgive our debtors as we are being forgiven of our debts, we find ourselves in the will of God and that is what matters the most. Obedience to God is what matters most of all.

"Extremes"

Be careful not to fall in the trap of extremes. It is very tempting to come out of a situation where you have to forgive and begin to operate in extremes. Most times when we are in these circumstances we might say, "I forgive them, but I will never..." I didn't finish that sentence because the end of that statement is unique to each of us. It might be that we say that we will never trust anyone or a particular person again. Or we might finish that sentence with never befriending people of a certain race or gender. We must not curse our futures because of what happened in our past. That is when you let the enemy win.

I was listening to Pastor Darius Daniels preach once, and he talked about how the thief or the enemy comes to "steal, kill and destroy." Some of you have read that scripture in John 10:10. He mentioned how we, most times, only look for him coming to destroy us or kill us, but we don't pay much attention to what he steals from us. We may have thought that the enemy was out to kill us, and prematurely celebrate that we are still here. Without looking to see if he came to steal instead. Do you still have your peace, your joy, or your sense of security? Is there anything missing? After it was all said and done, I was tempted to shut it all down with everyone that hurt me. I told my husband that I wouldn't divorce him, but that we had to be separated in this season. I didn't close that door. But when it came to her, I said to myself; there was no need for us to EVER talk again. It just wasn't necessary. However, God didn't feel the same.

"Making Room"

It's interesting how you can forget really significant happenings in your day until God reminds you, and ties everything together. I was running just "on time," which was making me nervous because if there was any traffic or any other delay, I would be late. So, I was hoping everything would be fine on the way to church. I was trying to be at church for sound check at 7am as I was going to be singing the lead for one of the songs in worship that Sunday. Being late, in my opinion, is not a good look as a leader. As I pulled out of the alley, something reminded me about "her" and what was done, and I shook my head. At the beginning, this happened fairly often. This was because once a week I was presented with the same challenge of having to be in the same space with the last person who hurt me the most. As usual, my process was this; to not think bad thoughts about her, affirm that she was forgiven, and if something new came up, I'd forgive her again for that. But this time, I tried to pray for her, and there was a hindrance. My intention was to pray that she be blessed.

That's what we are taught to do...right? We are supposed to bless and not curse. Well, that morning it was a problem, and I wasn't about to pass over it. Why? Because this had been bothering me for a while. I had been betrayed before, over and over. I had forgiven all the others, right away, just like I did her. I even went on a trip with one person that had hurt me in the past, recently. We had the best time! I couldn't figure out why this circumstance was so different. Why was I so bothered by her if I had forgiven her? I prayed to God in the car asking Him what really was the deal? Then it came to me. I didn't mind forgiving her. I believe we all deserve that grace. I was given that grace. BUT, in that moment, I realized that I didn't want her to be blessed. I didn't mind her being forgiven, but I had a problem with her being blessed. Even now, I'm reminded about how it bothered me to see her seemingly prosper in her business, and be quickly accepted and praised by our mutual friends, and colleagues. I had to sit and watch her still be with the young people that I was pastoring, while I couldn't because of their decisions. So yes, I had an epiphany that morning. In my heart, I didn't want the one who hurt me to be blessed, but in reality, I didn't want my sister in Christ to be blessed. Her identity is not what she did. Her identity is in Christ. I know this because my identity is not brokenness, my identity is being a child of God. So, this was a problem. This was a big problem. But the crazy thing is, I forgot all about this conversation with God by the time I got to church. I moved on. I started to rehearse the songs that we were going to sing for the rest of the drive to church. I want to be found faithful, right?

So, I was standing on stage and it was the last of the three services for the day. I wasn't dreading it. I was excited to see what God wanted to do in this service. It was time to be used by God to minister in song to a new set of people who needed God just as much as I did. I seriously count it a privilege. So, I was ready to hit it. The countdown finished and I welcomed everyone as the music started. I looked around as I greeted the people and I saw "her". I got thrown off. I was now annoyed that her presence had any effect on me, AND I was trying to get it together because in one second this song would start and I was leading it. I stumbled just a little as I began, but in my head, I was a straight intercessor going in, and praying on my behalf, and on behalf of everyone I was ministering to. I could not get off my assignment at that moment because of the mess I was in. God helped me focus and pull it together. I tried to not look that way as much because I just didn't want that on my mind as I lead people. It worked! God helped me to focus on the task at hand and helped me to really listen to Him. It was the last song and I love this song. We were singing "Make Room" by Evelyn and Lucas Cortazio.

Verse 1
Here is where I lay it down
Every burden every crown
This is my surrender. This is my surrender
Here is where I lay it down
Every lie and every doubt
This is my surrender

Chorus
And I will make room for you
To do whatever you want to
Do whatever you want to
And I will make room for you
To do whatever you want to
Do whatever you want to

I was standing there, leading people to lay down everything and make room for God. The Holy Spirit reminded me of our devotions that week, and how he called me out on being scared to have faith that my marriage was being healed. I didn't want to fully believe that would happen because I felt that it wasn't up to my belief or faith in God. I felt that it depended on my husband as well. He has free will. And this is true. But really, the issue was, I was protecting myself because I didn't want to look like a fool again (in my eyes). I didn't want to look like I was all in and get burned again. Even if I was all in. God brought up Hebrews 11:6 in my spirit. He didn't say where the scripture was found, but I was reminded of the line in the passage that says that "He is a rewarder of those who diligently seek Him." I had to google it to read the whole verse.

For the last two services, I kept hearing the words "Preconceived notions and outcomes." I felt pressed to share with the congregation during the song about my devotions that week, and that passage of scripture. But I got caught up in conversations between services and I didn't get to re-read that scripture verse so it would be fresh in my mind. So, on the spot, I had to make a choice, to ignore the tug on me to share because I didn't quite remember the scripture, or just open my mouth and see what God would do. I chose the latter. I initially started to say the scripture wrong, but then it came back to me. I shared that we should not put our faith in what we want God to do, or even in what God said He would do, but instead put our faith in God Himself. Hebrews 11:6 told us to believe that He IS, and that He is a rewarder of those who diligently seek Him. He didn't tell us what the reward was, but we should just believe in Him, and seek HIM.

I continued to minister the song, and then it happened. In the middle of the song, I saw myself talking to HER. In an effort to stay focused, I kept pressing through the song, desperate to hear God clearly about ministering the song, then He flipped it on me (while I was singing) and used the song to ask me if I was going to obey and lay it down. Urrrrgh!!!! Why would He ask me to do this, then convict me with the very song I was singing at that moment? While we were still on stage and my worship pastor/campus pastor was speaking, I began negotiating with God. "Can I just send a text?...What if I write a letter?" I just kept feeling convicted about my obedience. I felt like God was saying, you can't move forward in your ministry with this unresolved issue in your heart. When I got off that stage, I went directly to my office, hoping no one would see me or stop me, and plopped down on my office chair and cried! It almost became a physical feeling how much I didn't want to do what God was asking me to do. All I could get out of my mouth was, "I don't want to do this... I don't want to do this." Over and over, I repeated those words. I had no intention of having to deal with her in the foreseeable future. I would say I don't have to deal with her unless God says different, but I didn't want Him to say anything different... AT ALL!!

Well, He said "different", and I had to figure out how I was going to do what He was asking of me. I heard a friend who happened to be one of the altar prayer team members as they were passing by my office. I just called her name out loud. I wasn't sure if she heard me, and I also wasn't sure if I wanted her to have heard me. After a few seconds, she backed up to see if someone had called her name. I said I needed prayer, and as I was about to say why, I felt my eyes well up and my throat get tight. I had to hurry up and get it out, before I fell apart. I just said that God asked me to do something, and I don't want to do it. "I need prayer." She began to pray for me, that I would have the strength to be obedient and do what He was asking of me. Some of the prayer I can't remember, because the tears really started coming, and I don't like crying in front of people. I kept wiping and wiping so all the tears could be gone by time she finished praying, but each tear I wiped away was instantly replaced.

It was time for offering and we needed to sing one more song. I had moved on in my head because a young person needed time with me right after I was prayed for. So, I went into ministry and listening mode. That really helped me. I wasn't meditating on what I had to do, or what I was feeling. After ministering to the young lady, I went quickly to the stage. We sang the song, and it went on longer than expected because, praise God, two people were getting baptized. When we finally came to an end and the announcements were being made, I remembered what I had to do. In my humanity, I gave avoiding to do what God said, one last try. I thought to myself, if I go to put my mic away, she might get up to leave and I'll "miss" the opportunity. I had already mentioned to God that "If He creates an opportunity, I'll do it." This was my attempt to put it on God that the opportunity never came. Just ridiculous. It's crazy how much we can kick and scream against what God is NOT trying to do to us, but FOR us.

"Amen"....Well, this was it, it was either now or never. I started to walk, and there was a pull for me to go left off stage as normal and put my mic away, but I pushed in boldness to walk straight off the stage and directly to her. I just walked up and said, "Can I talk to you?"

This conversation wasn't about pouring out to her everything she did, and how I felt. God simply wanted me to tell her that she was released. That she didn't have to walk into the church still feeling tied to what she did. I was honest, that I didn't want to have this conversation, and that it was still something I was dealing with, but that regardless, she was released. Earlier that morning, I felt that God wanted me to pray for her. I had already forgiven her, but I couldn't bless her that morning. I didn't want her to be blessed. I found myself acting like Jonah. Jonah was sent on an assignment to a people that were in sin, and he didn't want to go minister to them because he knew they would accept his message and be blessed. He ran the other way and God wasn't having it. It didn't go well. There was a boat...he was tossed into the water... there was a fish. Things got intense. BUT in the end, he was obedient. Jesus taught us and showed us how to pray "Not my will but yours be done." I pray this ALL the time. In this situation, I had to put my money where my mouth was. I had to put actions to my prayers.

We must not be so quick to say never. We must leave room for God to be God. Don't go to the extreme and begin saying everything that you will and will not do from now on. Keep your heart surrendered to God and keep a "Not my will but yours be done" in your spirit.

CHAPTER EIGHT

Two Things

When I was headed to my mentor and his wife's home, I prayed all the way there. As I spoke to them and they listened, it was like God was speaking to me through me. I shared with them my conversations with God about what we hadn't done to fix this marriage each time there was an "incident." I told them there were two things that weren't done consistently that I would need to see to consider ending the separation. Those two things were time and counseling. We always rushed back into "normalcy" after there was any kind of incidence. There wasn't healing, or intentional addressing of the true underlying issues. We would put a Band-Aid on it and end up in the same places. These issues that we had, needed more than 'let's work on how we talk to each other.' These issues we had were bigger than our marriage completely. We needed counseling to deal with our souls. I mentioned to them that our marriage wasn't the sickness, it was just a symptom. It was just the innocent bystander that got shot for being at the wrong place at the wrong time.

When I mentioned those two things to them, it's like I got clarity from God on my task at hand. I had a Word for moving forward, and it was those two things, time and counseling. I wasn't going to trust anything else in this process. I couldn't trust anything else. When I left their place I actually felt better. They listened. They prayed for me. They didn't assume to know what path I needed to take in my unique situation. Apparently, other people don't have the same story as me. When they went to their pastors or mentors, they were given bad or generic advice. They were told to go home and stay with their man or you need to divorce. This is unfortunate that godly leaders would not go to God about what to do in a situation involving HIS children. I know that I am blessed because I was heard, was given Biblical truths, and the pressure was released from me to do one thing or another.

Life after Thanksgiving, finding out that I'm not crazy, and having a plan of "two things" were interesting to say the least. I eventually told my mother and she took it well. She was encouraging by offering her understanding, and Bible scriptures to bring me through this tough time. I hate that my mom had to see me hurt, or crying, and trying to maintain. I hate that my mom had to see me try to explain why we were not going home and to protect the image of my husband in my son's eyes at the same time. I don't know about anyone else but, our son is super smart, so I know he was trying to process everything that he was experiencing. My mother had to see all of it. But on the other hand, I was able to listen to her wisdom, and she was also able to see me enact the "Me Plan."

The "Me Plan" was what my mother taught me about taking care of myself. Through this journey, I discovered I had treated myself so badly, by what I had allowed, but also by putting myself last. I wasn't taking care of myself.

There were health issues that I could have dealt with, but I put them on the back burner to deal with home.

Being honest about my shortcomings and my weaknesses didn't keep me as embarrassed as I thought. Don't get me wrong, it was embarrassing! But, it was not nearly as bad as I expected. It actually brought me freedom. I didn't have to hide behind a mask of "I got it together" anymore. And once I started to get my confidence back, and an appreciation for me, I began to do things for myself that I hadn't done at all or in years. It's interesting how powerful the small things can be. I went to Burlington and bought a winter coat, hat, scarf, and gloves. These are simple things, but I hadn't even done something like this for myself. My confidence and comfortability with myself grew. I went without makeup for a while because I just wanted to be comfortable with exactly who I was and how I looked for a while. It was almost like a rebirth. The biggest thing I did was walk right into what I believe is some of God's call for my life. I finally started my own business, I Investments LLC. This company was the epitome of my new life and my new message, of women investing in themselves so they can invest in others.

I still had moments where I realized how deep things had gotten for me in my head. While I was at Burlington, I was looking for a winter coat for our son. There was a coat I liked but I found myself hindered and almost paralyzed to make a decision, because of what I thought my husband would think of the coat. I realized I had unhealthy constraints, that left me feeling like I was always walking on eggshells, and I couldn't make a mistake. This mindset is the makings of living in your head and being a people pleaser.

In my experience on this journey, I had so many kind people let us know they had been through similar situations and offered advice. They were encouraging and offered to have lunch with us all the time. It was such a great show of the Body of Christ stepping up and loving on the broken. In addition to this response, I also got a lot of people telling me what they think was right, and what I should do. After hearing all the voices, the good, the great and the bad, I began to feel confused and stressed out. I was trying to hear God and I had all these voices of well-meaning people in my head. It was too much! My sister saw that this was the case and sent me away to the Abbey Resort in Wisconsin for a night. This was the best gift I could have received at this time. I love going on road trips by myself. I always have a good time because I can hear God so clearly and we have fun clowning in the car together. We are like two old friends with inside jokes, in the car.

Before I could even get to the resort, I had heard from God and he gave me so much clarity. While I was out there, I stepped out on faith and started the process of forming my business and began to get vision for what I was supposed to do, and how I was supposed to be in this season. But when I came down from the "mountain" things got not so clear.

I started counseling for myself right away. I was not trying to repeat my old life again. I needed to get to the bottom of why I made the choices that I did and why I allowed myself to be manipulated for years. I needed to know why I couldn't act on my convictions. The counseling was very helpful because I was able to talk. I often find that no one "really" wants to hear what I have to say about me. But I get it. It is difficult to sit and listen to people's hurts, and inner thoughts, if you are not getting something out of it. It is hard for people to give their time with nothing in return. I hear people talk about it all the time. We as humans only want to be in give and take relationships. I understand this, because I desire the same thing. But there is always a need for give-only relationships and receive-only relationships. Notice I didn't say take-only relationships. There is a big difference between receiving and taking. One is healthy and necessary in life, and the other is unhealthy and can be a cancer to someone's life.

The best way I could describe the need for one-way relationships is with bodies of water. When you only have a two-way relationship, you can become like a lake that is totally enclosed, and stagnant. There is no water coming in nor out. It is two people that are not receiving outside of this relationship individually, but giving to each other. There is no fresh water coming in. No revelation or much growth. It is just the same old, same old. Have you experienced that? I have. I have had relationships and even went to churches where there was no newness. We just did the same things, and we were not growing because we just held on to what we had. But when you add one-way relationships to your life, you become like a river that continuously gets refreshed and is able to support a two-way relationship. You can give to others when you are being poured into, without the responsibility of giving to the one who is giving to you. You have more to offer your two-way relationships when you are receiving and changing. There is a need for each of us to pour out what is in us, so we have room to receive more. It is the way God designed us. We spend extended seasons in relationships with our parents that is a one-way relationship (not to say there aren't two-way moments or lessons). But when they are receiving and growing healthily, they are able to give to us consistently. You see, parents and anyone can burnout when they constantly give but are not in position (or in a relationship) to receive.

Unfortunately (but also fortunately), there was a lack of people around me that was in a place where they could just listen and just give, and not receive from me. I say that it was fortunate as well, because I was in a place where I needed to be running to God as my refuge and not everyone else. This is extremely uncomfortable for me because I am one that is both introverted and extroverted. I'm a shy extrovert, and a bunch of other labels. I am the one that usually falls right in the middle of those personality quizzes and tests. I have a need to be around people to refuel, but I also have a need to be by myself to refuel and self-evaluate as well. I am very introspective when alone, but my gifts offer introspection to others on very extroverted platforms. There are times when I want to be around people, but God needs me to be with Him. It is a balance (or off balance) type of deal. The balance is not even. God desires me to need Him more than others. So, there are times when people conveniently disappear when I *think* I need them the most. But what is usually happening is God knows what I really need at that time, and what is needed is more of Him. Whenever I am looking for peace, validation, or acceptance from others, God has to reign it in, redirect my focus, and limit my access to people. It is an act of love to deter me from seeking fulfillment from sources that cannot supply my needs.

I went to a Christian counselor. The first counselor I had gave me the wrong vibe, because she was too angry about what happened to me. She was verbally expressing her disdain for my husband's actions. I felt like she wasn't being objective. I didn't need someone to just be a yes woman for me and agree on my notions about why things are the way that they are. I needed someone submitted to the Holy Spirit that could do some digging and help me see what was going on inside of me and give me practical ways to change my behavior.

However, I struggled with the counseling because I couldn't get myself to act on what I knew I needed to do or say. We would discuss conversations that I needed to have with my husband or actions that I could take, but I couldn't muster the courage or strength to do any of it. Why? Why was I unable to do the things that would cause me to grow and change? Why couldn't I do my assignments in counseling?

When I left my home and my husband, I was unaware of the amount of complicated emotions I was going to feel and have to work through. I had my instructions of "two things," but I also had crazy emotions every day and challenges along the way in my communication—with my husband, my son, and the outside world. Some of the feelings that came up were concerns about not knowing who knew what, every time I set foot in my church. As I walked through the hallways, what were people thinking? I could handle it if they were talking to me, but I was wondering what were the conversations that were being had about me and my life.

I dealt with the feelings of pressure to be healed now, or to at least look like healing was happening now. I think that some people's desire, and my own desire to see the testimony left little room for the size of the test that was at hand. Sometimes we can expect one-size fits all victories. Not all marriages that are experiencing issues or people that are going through, travel the same path to their victory and healing. There are some experiences that just have to be lived through. Some victories come quick, and others take time, for various reasons. Those reasons are not always disobedience or lack of faith. Time in itself is a test, and it was on my two things list. But it is the one thing that I failed at.

Loneliness was a common thing for me to experience. A lot of my life I felt lonely. The age gap between myself and my siblings brought about a level of loneliness. The fact that I was saved at a young age brought about loneliness. There were so many things that brought about loneliness in my life, but it just seemed to feel so much bigger in this tumultuous season of my life. I often laid down at night time on the air mattress next to my mother's bed in my sister's house, crying to myself and hoping my mom couldn't see or hear it.

All these feelings, that were unexpected, or unexpected on this level, brought about a desire to hurry through this fire season. When I needed to stay in the fire to get purified and strengthened, I wanted out. It was almost like a secret desire that even my own mind didn't pick up on. Because this was the case, I reinterpreted progress to mean healing. Moving forward doesn't equal healing. You can move forward without getting healed. I reinterpreted progress to be healing simply because I wanted it to be so, and everyone else wanted it to be so as well. Have you ever just been tired of being in the same test or situation? You think to yourself that no one wants to see this or hear about this anymore. They are over it. I just wanted to rush to the end of the book. I wanted to get to the testimony. I wanted to arrive at my happily ever after, before I got all that I needed from the test.

My husband began to fight for the marriage, at a time when we needed to fight for ourselves individually. He bought me flowers and food, and took me out. It was from a well-intentioned place in his heart, it just wasn't what I needed at that time. I saw these efforts as my escape from the drama. Even though I knew there were two things I needed to see, counseling and time. I gave into the relief of my loneliness. I sacrificed the completion of my healing, and the equipment of more strength, for relief. I welcomed the feelings of being wanted and family because it felt good, but what I really needed was time. I needed time to practice the spiritual and natural disciplines it takes to walk through your healing and stay healed.

So, after a while, even though I was going to counseling, I was being disobedient to the second instruction I feel God gave me...time. I didn't give it time. When it all went down, I was able to speak up for myself, and say everything I needed to say. I felt incredible freedom, and peace for the first time in a long time. But once I came back home, I stunted my growth by not giving myself time to practice the disciplines that I needed to stay healed. Therefore, I ended up retreating back into my head and living there. I no longer had the strength nor courage to speak up. I went back to old habits, but now the new battle was the regret of coming back to soon.

PART THREE:

Becoming Savage

CHAPTER NINE

Fighting The Casket

I never knew that regret could have such an impact on someone's life. Regret began to take over my life, because it was taking over my speech. When I talked about where I was at with my counselors, regret would come pouring out. "I shouldn't have come back so soon." I felt I had ruined my one chance at changing this marriage and becoming free from the bondage I felt within my own self at home. I went back to a place that held the memories of the silence, manipulation, and feeling like I was crazy. I looked at the pictures on the wall and they would piss me off, because I felt like they were all fake memories. I would think back to most of those moments, and how before, during, or after that picture was taken, I felt diminished, or unwanted, or like I was forcing this idea of family and closeness. I didn't like this place. The piling clothes and dishes were a picture of the piling regret and frustration I felt for still being *there*.

I was living in this house, but I had checked out. I returned not to the old me, but to the old habits of living inside my head and giving up on speaking out about anything. I felt defeated because "I failed." I came back. These are the thoughts that swirled around in my head whether I was talking to someone or not. I had constant reminders of these feelings. I loved my son, but I despised "coming home." I would linger after work events and talk with people because I didn't want to go home. Home wasn't a place of peace for me. I had it in my head that it was a place that just reminded me of my failure. I was stuck.

During the course of about a year, I hadn't even taken the things out of my trunk from when I left. There were things still at my sister's house from when I left. The items that went into my trunk from the day I had to clear my office out was still in my trunk. I was literally carrying with me, everywhere I went, the pain and frustration of what happened to me.

Our marriage consisted of us living together, and keeping our same routine of working. We came home and wouldn't really talk, then watch our shows after our son went to bed. As we watched tv we would talk about the show and laugh, but deep inside it frustrated me that our relationship was so surface. We would not truly communicate about much of anything. Sometimes we would have four loaves of bread because we both went out and bought it, or both of us would get the same thing for Brenden that he needed, because we wouldn't talk. We lived together but did our own thing.

I kept looking at the issues of our marriage again and again. Doing this would trigger me to feelings of hopelessness and numbness. I would be distracted by the array of feelings and it fluctuated all the time. I kept beating myself up because "I failed," because I went back. I felt weak.

In my heart, I kept rehearsing the two things God told me that I didn't follow through with. I couldn't get past it. I kept saying from the time everything went down, that our marriage needed to die, not be restored. And there is some truth to that, but what I didn't comprehend was that it was really the people in the marriage who needed to die.

One day at work, a lady who later became a mentor to me, must have asked how I was doing. I shared with her cautiously and without revealing everything. She saw that I was dealing with a lot of regret. It was pouring out of me with each sentence. It was in my countenance. When I first left home, my looks changed. I had a disposition of freedom and joy about me. I had been released from a lot of things, and I looked and felt lighter. Now, in this conversation you can see I had new weights on me. I was burdened once again.

I remember she told me about this scripture that I had heard before but didn't apply to this situation or my life. This scripture has ended up being brought back up repeatedly by different people and prophets that don't know each other. She recited to me John 12:24. Jesus says, "I tell you the truth, unless a kernel of wheat is planted in the soil and dies, it remains alone. But its death will produce many new kernels—a plentiful harvest of new lives" NLT.

My husband and I couldn't produce in our marriage or walk in God's will unless we died. Seeds can be eaten, or they can be planted and then many can eat. My life wouldn't have been a waste if I had just left and lived my best life. I alone would have benefited, and God wants me to benefit. BUT, the confessions of my heart and my mouth has always been to serve God with my life. And His will for my life was not to live, eat, be merry and die, but to help others along the way to have the opportunity to live, eat and be merry too. God's desire for our lives doesn't stop with us.

This lady, over time, by the Holy Spirit, helped me to understand that all this time I was trying to "fight the casket." I was trying to navigate living, when all the while I needed to be dying. I needed to die to myself and let go of who I thought I was going to be. I needed to let the fantasies, that match the world's view of success and strength, die. I needed to let my expectations for marriage die.

The regretful, vengeful, hopeless, bitter person needed to die. During the course of a year after everything blew up, I started my business I Investments LLC, but I did nothing with it because I had not yet died. I needed to get out of the way and make room for God. This was not my marriage; it was God's marriage. We had taken the reins of what He had put together. This marriage and our individual lives had to be back in His care. God had to be back in charge of my life. My thoughts and decisions had to be governed by the Holy Spirit, and not my hurt or expectations.

I couldn't and cannot force anyone else to die, but I had to make up in my mind that I was going to die. I left all the distractions behind and I focused on the will of God for my life, that I was neglecting because of the distractions. Fighting the casket had me all the way distracted from my purpose. It is in death that I was able to see again. Isn't that crazy! God is so mysterious.

I began to bring everything to God. If I was triggered, I asked God how I should respond. It brought me so much peace because I saw myself changing. Instead of getting a text, and it thrust me into depression, I would pause and give it to God. When a financial issue would arise, I started off with an immediate freak-out. Then it changed where I would take a few minutes before I would freak-out. Finally, I just stopped freaking out. I stopped trying to fix everything myself. I quit attempting to come up with solutions. The weight of the world was beginning to lift.

My real death came when I gave up my sleep in the mornings and gave them to God. The more I became aware of the calling I was forsaking, and the lives I was affecting by not walking in that calling, I decided to die by any means necessary. Now, sleep means a lot to me. I figured that out when I had my son, and I saw the levels of anger I felt because I had to get up from my sleep, over and over again. I obviously was not angry with my son; I was just mad that I had to miss sleep.

I went from never being able to get up for anything unless it was work, school, or something fun I wanted to do, to getting up about 5am to pray, seek God about everything, and work on the ministry and business God gave me to steward. I was so impressed by this miracle. I say miracle because it is a legit miracle. This had never consistently happened before. I had to do whatever was necessary to stay on course and die to myself. When I wake up and the negotiations start with myself..."Five more minutes," "Let's do 6am today," "Let's find time later in the day," I ask myself if this sleep is worth more than my family, my future, or the people who need what God has placed inside of me.

WHAT I DID WRONG IN FIGHTING
THE CASKET FOR 12 YEARS

Hiding Place

In twelve years of fighting the casket, what did I do wrong? Well, I lived in my head. This was like my hiding place. This is where I could scream, be negative, and say what I really wanted to say HOW I really wanted to say it. Instead of supporting myself by speaking out, I lived in this headspace of insecurity, comparison, and denial. This was toxic living and it became a habit, until I decided to die.

Self-Sacrifice

I surrendered to self-sacrifice, which I thought was love. I thought I was loving like Jesus by sacrificing my life. But I later learned that love really is obedience. Jesus was being obedient to the cross (Philippians 2:8). And I was disobedient in my relationship in what I was supposed to do, who I was supposed to be, and who I was supposed to serve. I ended up being the opposite. God commissioned me to speak out, but I was silent.

The Trap

I surrendered to the feeling of being trapped in my marriage. I was giving into the overwhelming thoughts and concept that I made a mistake in accepting this treatment and marrying this person. I felt like I was just going to have to put my head down and endure the years, living in my head. I was living in an opportunity for God's glory, but I surrendered to the "trapped" mindset.

Asking for Permission

I found out by re-reading emails and rehashing conversations we had in the past, that I would talk and write about going back to being separated. I was doing all that because I was looking for permission to be obedient to the two things, I believed that God said to me (time and counseling). I was too scared to just be obedient in what I thought God was saying, no matter how many times it would come back around to me.

WHAT I DID RIGHT IN FIGHTING THE CASKET FOR 12 YEARS

Pro-Forgiver

I became a professional at forgiving. Since I had so many times to practice, I learned how to forgive quickly, and then go seek my healing. I forgave repeatedly when I would discover another way that I was affected by what happened.

Sought Healing

At first, I was not seeking my healing the right way. But then I figured out what I was doing wrong. I was trying to rush to the end of the testimony. I had to feel the deep pain of the trauma and explore how it changed me, so I could get healed in those places as well.

Trusted the Holy Spirit

I started trusting the Holy Spirit in me again. Previously, questioning whether or not I was crazy, had me not trusting my spiritual gifts or that I was hearing from God. I used to think that if all of this drama is what I got from marrying someone I thought God said was my husband, maybe I was wrong. But I don't think that way anymore. I had to trust that I hear God correctly, and I hear Him even in storms.

Healing in the Wilderness

I submitted to HEALING IN THE WILDERNESS. When the Children of Israel were exiled to Babylon (Jeremiah 29), they were told by Jeremiah that they were not coming out soon. He told them to prosper right where they are. I had to build my muscles in the wilderness. I think about the Rocky movies when he didn't have the fancy, sanitized gyms nor equipment to train for the big fight. He went into nature and used it to train. He used tires and ran on the street. He didn't use an air-conditioned indoor track.

I had to learn my lessons and build myself up in the fire. In the wilderness, I am building endurance, guarding my heart, developing habits of focus, and weakening judgmental behavior. I am staying motivated to walk in my purpose regardless of what's going on around me. I am trusting in the Holy Spirit in ME and bearing the fruit of self-discipline. And I am becoming more self-sufficient in regard to having the disciplines and the finances to take care of myself. This is not to emasculate my husband; it is about me not being in a position of demise and making sure I am bringing my best self to my family. The Proverbs 31 woman was self- sufficient. Husband and wife had their own things going on and it was a good thing. This is not to knock or devalue anyone else's life setup, or instructions from God. This is just what God was doing in me. This is how I stopped fighting the casket and began to be the wheat that was planted to die, and then bring forth many seeds.

CHAPTER TEN

My Success Story

So, what is my success story? Was it that I was back-stabbed, everything fell apart, but I pulled myself up by my own bootstraps and built a ten-figure business? No. I did and do have success, but it looks differently than what you see on social media or tv. My real success is that I'm becoming SAVAGE.

You might be wondering what that means. Well, let me first tell you what it doesn't mean. Becoming savage is not about shifting your focus on yourself. It is not about getting fed up finally and determining that, from now on, I am just taking care of myself and myself alone. Honestly, caring for myself alone was not enough. It didn't satisfy like you would think it would. But when my care for God was increased over my care for myself (which is included), I really started to become savage. I processed that all that happened, including my distractions, was not okay with God. This was not the life He intended for me, nor was leading me to.

Thinking about these things caused me to realize that I was sitting on almost everything God was giving me to do. I saw how I would start things (like my business), then because of my circumstances, I would get depressed or insecure. Walking in disobedience will affect you greatly.

I saw the strength I already had in me to have a strong mind. I put the work in intentionally. What needed to change was the double mindedness. I couldn't be an enabler and still have peace. I couldn't live in my head, keeping everything to myself, and still maintain my strong mind. I couldn't put myself last and expect my business to grow and flourish at the same time.

So, how do I become savage? And I say "become" because this is an ongoing process that can't be rushed. You can become savage in every aspect of your life, and at every stage of your life. So, what did I do and am I doing, to become savage?

"Work My Plan"

One morning I woke up at my brother's house. I was visiting for Thanksgiving in Indy. This was a much happier Thanksgiving, before I was married. I went downstairs to do my devotions on the couch by myself and God just gave me a download. This is where He just gives me something basically in its entirety. I have had song downloads, or book outline downloads, but this time it was a program. I think it was originally called Head to Toe Coaching. But thank God for His wisdom over time, and a friend with creativity. The program "The Strong Mind" was created on that couch.

Little did I know that I was going to have to walk out this program myself on a daily basis. In The Strong Mind, you learn about the popular head conversations that we all have that are unhealthy and hindering us. It deals with why or how we can go to church on a regular basis, love God, and still struggle. The best part is it includes action plans, so we are making changes in our lives. I had a plan that I thought was for others (and it is), but really it was for my mental transformation (Romans 12:2). I had to work my plan! I couldn't live with gold and not spend it. I had to use the tools God gave me to help others, to help myself.

One of the terms I use in The Strong Mind is called "listing." This is where you are triggered to list in your mind all the things that are going wrong. The things on the list are true and real. The issue with listing is not whether or not what your listing is true, but that it is off balance. Most of our lists are 10% of our lives, but they get painted as if they are the whole 100%. This is inaccurate and puts our minds in an unwarranted state of anxiety. The real rest of the 90% is filled with the daily blessings of God we don't even think about or acknowledge. I got caught up in "listing". It is a strong temptation. But I had to work my plan. I already had action plans, but I had to use them.

One of my action plans is my "SBS Plan." When I am tempted to go off, when I am tempted to begin listing, or if I have a thought that usually leads to depression or anxiety I "SBS." I "STOP, BREATHE and SAY." I stop myself in my own tracks, I take a deep breath, then I begin to say to myself what I am not about to do. For example, I was coming home from work and feeling good, but when I began to pull up to my home and parked, I was triggered. I began to feel all the negative feelings that wanted to turn into listing how it is going to be or feel when I get inside.

I had to literally stop that train of thought, breathe, and say to myself, "No one can change my atmosphere except for me." I am not a thermometer; I am a thermostat. I may not have control of everyone else, but the Holy Spirit gave me self-control of this one right here, me. And I began to say how it was going to be, instead of what I "might" feel, and what "could" happen. Oftentimes I have to SBS when I am tempted to speak, when I really need to pray. Lately, it has been short and sweet. I get triggered, and I simply say, "I'm not going." I've decided that I'm not boarding that train. I know where it is headed, and "I'm not going."

"SBS" really is just capturing every thought, casting down everything that isn't right, and deciding what I am going to think about, or not going to think about (2 Corinthians 10:5, Philippians 4:8). I can't let my thoughts and emotions have control of this train. Becoming savage means, I have to work my plans, my Biblically based plans. I'm not interested in just good ideas. It is the God idea or plan that will work for me.

"Untamed by This World"

For years I wanted to be liked and accepted by people. This desire has created cracks in my armor; spaces for worldliness to get through. In order to maintain this desire, you have to really change who you are. There is a level of becoming, or conforming, to what the world deems as acceptable or likeable. I am unable to follow Jesus when I am chasing acceptance from the world. Becoming savage means, I am becoming untamed by this world.

I cannot not live by the standards of this world. I thought I wasn't conforming until I noticed that I was comparing myself to others just like the world; and tempted to be led by my feelings just like the world. I even became impatient, wanting everything now including complete healing.

Becoming savage meant I needed to reject what the world says I should do. With the story that I have, the world would have wanted me to hate my husband and "her". The world would have suggested that I throw both of them under several buses on social media. Was I tempted to do so? Absolutely...often. I was also tempted to drink my pain and embarrassment away. I can see myself when I was in stores passing the liquor isles, having to SBS. I was tempted to run away from it all and leave everyone hanging. I was tempted to go find someone else *real quick* to make me feel wanted and desired temporarily.

These are all worldly temptations that would have had me tamed by the world's standards. But, "I'm not going!" If I want Kingdom promises, and Kingdom results, I need to live untamed by this world. I rejected all these temptations because I decided to live for God's will being done in me, and not live for my feelings and instant satisfaction or revenge. I decided I was going to be different, even if it meant standing alone.

"Unleashing Wild Faith"

Let me just say it. During and after this season, I will be an amazing mother, wife, businesswoman, teacher, and friend. I had to realize I CAN do this. My faith is not in my abilities, but it is in God and what He said is His will for my life. I am the head and not the tail, I am above and not beneath (Deuteronomy 28:13). I intentionally get motivated daily to foster this wild faith. I watch videos to encourage myself. I listen to songs to bring me out of a funk. I believe in myself and take action. And that may be for business or for home. I do things to prepare myself and put myself out there to be a part of God's will.

I ACTED on my faith. I had to decide to believe in God's Word for my life. God made me a teacher, so I need to be teaching and/or growing in my gift to teach. I started investing in what I know to be true about God's will for me. That is why I started my business I Investments LLC. I wanted to create opportunities for women to invest in themselves so that they can invest in others. God took a calculated chance and invested in me. He gave me gifts and talents, but it doesn't stop there. Now, I must invest in myself.

When we feed our trees, they bear fruit. This fruit is not just for you to eat but it is for others to enjoy. We invest in ourselves so we can invest in others. I challenge you to find out God's will for your life. Pray, and even look at what He already has put inside of you. Feed that gift or talent. Invest in it even if it is something you don't want right now. I didn't want to be a speaker, preacher, or anything that was out and in front of people. I wanted to use my gifts but didn't want to be the center of attention. I was shy, and the thought of doing these things made me nervous and self-conscious. However, I couldn't deny that my gifts were a part of God's will for my life.

I didn't start just believing in myself, I began to unleash *wild faith* in God; that His will for my life was going to come to pass. He was my promise! It wasn't about me. My desire was to see God pleased with my life and decisions, and that requires me to unleash my wild and crazy faith that what He said... WILL happen. I will be healed. I will walk in my purpose and financial freedom. I will be free!

"Uncovering the Treasures Within"

I am a teacher, a speaker, a worshipper, and a writer. These and more are all treasures that are inside of me. I have to do and be what God created me to do and be. There are treasures on the inside of all of us that we should uncover. There is satisfaction found in the treasure God seeded in us.

I remember deciding to go ahead and host a life group using the program God gave me, The Strong Mind. It was our first gathering together. I talked and they shared. It was great. But when I finished and was on my way home, I frantically called my sister and mom. I was trying to find someone to listen to me share this great feeling I felt. I felt FULL. I sat in that car and thought to myself, *"This must be what Jesus meant when He said His meat was to do the will of God."* I was finally walking in my calling and I felt satisfied. This is what I needed to be doing for the rest of my life. Teaching, speaking and engaging with people in the midst of their real-life circumstances, by sharing mine. I've never felt that elated or fulfilled by something I had done. It felt so good.

There are treasures inside of you that will bless you when you share them. But the greatest treasure that can be inside of you that you must share uniquely is Jesus. He is the light shining in your heart, that others need to meet and experience through you (2 Corinthians 4:7). I must say this "out loud" so that we always know that the great power we possess comes from God and not ourselves. I know this is contrary to what the world says. The world will have you believing everything you need is in you. But if you haven't recognized that God is the "everything you need," you don't have anything you need already in you.

I define becoming savage as a person who is becoming untamed by this world, unleashing wild faith and is uncovering their treasures within. This is my secret sauce! This is the foundation of my missions out here in this world. I wrote this book so that you can decide to start becoming savage with me. I am not inviting you to a 3-step program that will fix all your problems. I am inviting you to become who God created you to be; an individual who savagely seeks to bring God glory. Will you accept this invitation?

"Why Did I Write This Book?"

After that crazy Thanksgiving, I felt pressed on every side by my troubles, but I wasn't crushed. I definitely was perplexed, but I didn't give in to despair. I felt like "Why me?" but I NEVER felt, nor was I, abandoned by God. Man! I was knocked down over and over again, but I was not destroyed. I learned that through my suffering I was presented with a unique opportunity to participate in the death of Jesus, so that the life of Jesus would be displayed in my life.

So, I will continue to teach, preach and sing, because I believe God. And because I believe God, I write. I do all of this for your benefit. I am thankful because, by the grace of God, the more people who read this book and are changed, will produce more and more glory to God. This is why I won't give up. Even though this season was killing me, my spirit was and is being renewed every day. For my current troubles won't last very long, but let me tell you, they WILL produce a glory that completely outweighs anything I've been through and will last forever. This fruit will REMAIN.

So, my wish for you is this, that you don't look at your present troubles and "list." Remove your focus from the things you can see, and rather fix your eyes on the things you can't see. For the things you see now, my friends, will be over soon, but the things you cannot see will last forever. These sentiments that I feel originally came from Paul's heart in 2 Corinthians 4:8-10, 13, 15-18. His words so well describe how I feel.

Let's start becoming savage! If you don't have a relationship with God through Jesus, and you want to know the God that brought me through all that I went through and transformed me into a savage woman, then I want to present some really good news to you.

Well, let me start off with the bad news first. You may have heard that God created this world, and the first humans he created were named Adam (a man), and Eve (a woman). They had everything but got tricked and disobeyed God. Because they disobeyed, they were separated from God, and Man has been separated from God ever since. However, God didn't want to be separated, but He had rules. Part of those rules is that the price of sinning or missing God's mark is death, BUT to satisfy that rule He made a big sacrifice. He sent His son to be born on earth, he experienced every temptation we do and have, but He never sinned. God sent His son so that He could pay the price for ALL of our sins once and for all, and with this payment we can be reconciled back in relationship with God. So, Jesus did just that and died the most horrific death to pay for our sins.

So, here's the GOOD NEWS. Yes, everyone has sinned, and the price of sin is death. But Jesus died that terrible death to pay for our sins, and God raised Him back to life on the third day with all power in Him. And now, if you confess out loud that Jesus is the Lord of your life (like a landlord or the one in charge of your life), and believe in your heart that God raised Jesus from being dead, you will be saved from paying the price of your sins.

If you want, you can pray this prayer with me.

"God, I know I am not perfect, and that means I have missed your mark. In other words, I have sinned against you. Please forgive me of my sins. I let go of my old life and willingly place my life into your charge. I confess that you are MY Lord and my Savior. You are now in charge of my life, and not me or any enemy of yours. I will now live for you and live in such a way that gives you glory. I don't know you well, but I commit to learning about you by reading the Bible and talking to you every day. Thank you so much for saving me from eternal death, and giving me real life. No matter what may come in life, you are my Lord, forever!"

I celebrate with you, and the Bible says heaven celebrates with you as well. This is literally the most important day of your life. Tell someone what you did today and stand firm on your belief in Jesus.

Now you can start your journey of becoming savage.

CHAPTER ELEVEN

My Calling

Has my story helped you overcome in any way? Are there lessons that I learned that helped you in your life circumstances? I would love to hear about it. One, it encourages me, and two, it helps me help others that need to hear this message. Reach out to me on social media and share your story with me.

Do you need to create and work your plan? Do you need help with your thoughts and mindsets and maybe still struggle with negativity silently? Do you live in your head like I did? I want to help you, on a practical level and let the Word of God give you a strong mind.

You may be still processing what you've been through and the mistakes that you have made that you don't know what to do with. It is common to feel defeated because of your failures. I want to help you move forward, and extract what you need going forward from your past experiences.

Do you have a story that needs to be told? Are you sitting on the lessons you learned that could change someone else's life, and help them overcome? Do not be a bad steward of the story God gave you. I want to help you get it out. Since 2004, I have felt the call to help people to share their testimonies. I have seen young ladies and seasoned women let their guards down and seek healing because someone shared their story. I want to see that happen over and over again, until I leave this world. I want to see that happen with you.

I think we need to talk. Myself and my team want to hear where you are at and where you want to go. If you want to become savage, I want to connect with you. I have groups, programs, and coaching all designed to fulfill my calling to help you. If you are ready to take action, and not just think about it or talk about it, let's have a discovery call to see how I can help you start becoming savage.

My Last Words...

"There's no shadow You won't light up, mountain You won't climb up, coming after me...

There's no wall you won't kick down, Lie You won't tear down coming after me."

Lyrics of "Reckless Love" by Cody Carnes

I never knew how far God would go to love me. I'll probably never really know everything that He has done. But I know it much better now than ever before. And my response to His love is the beautiful lyrics to Make Room by Evelyn and Lucas Cortazio.

Here is where I lay it down, Every burden, every crown

This I my surrender. This is my surrender

Here is where I lay it down, Every Lie and Every Doubt

This is my surrender

And I will make room for you…To do whatever you want to…"